MY
DISCOVERY
OF
ENGLAND

ELIMINÉ

D1479779

Stephen Leacock

MY
DISCOVERY
OF
ENGLAND

Introduction : George Whalley

General Editor : Malcolm Ross

New Canadian Library No. 28

MC CLELLAND AND STEWART LIMITED

PRINTED AND BOND IN CANADA BY
T. H. BEST PRINTING COMPANY LIMITED

CONTENTS

Stephen Leacock arrived in England in late September
1921 to make his first professional lecture tour. The pub-
lication of his *Literary Lapses* in 1910 and of ten books
in the following ten years had won a wide celebrity for
him in England and the United States, and some recognition in his own country. *The Times* welcomed him
on arrival as "a master of satire." On this tour he spoke
a few times "on serious subjects" at the universities, at
business gatherings, and at London dinners; but for the
main part of his tour he depended upon two lectures—
"Frenzied Fiction" and "Drama As I See It"—made up
from previously published material. These he presented
in fifty appearances between October 4 and December
23, going "as far north as Aberdeen and as far south as
Brighton and Bournemouth . . . eastward to Ipswich
and westward into Wales." Leacock's agent did not
fail to provide him with official encouragement: at his
London lectures he was introduced in turn by the editors
of *Punch*, the *Westminster Gazette*, *The Times*, and
the *Spectator*. The tour brought his annual income for
the first time above $20,000; it also provided him with
the material for his next annual volume. He had noticed
with what prompt and lucrative facility English literary
men turned into writing their first impressions of Amer-

ica. He himself had been born in England but had come to Canada as a child; he had visited England in 1907 as a young political science professor lecturing on "Imperial Organization" under the auspices of the Rhodes Trust. He decided now to "restore the balance of trade" in "Impressions" by writing, under the assumed privilege of slight acquaintance, a comic survey of England, her people, beliefs, manners, and institutions. Unlike some writers of "impressions" he could, he said, draw if necessary "upon observations extending over fourteen years."

My Discovery of England consists of ten sketches in a mixed manner which is neither consistently satire nor parody. The three first chapters unfold against the background of the ocean crossing, the landing in Liverpool, the rail journey to London, his first interviews with the English press, his solitary but irresolute exploration of London (the Tower, the British Museum, the Abbey). Stephen Leacock seems to have brought home almost as little of England as those resolute tourists of our own day who endanger their respiration if not their health with an intricate cross-gartering of camera straps, light meters, and long-focus lenses. But that is all part of the fun. The best travel books (he might argue) are those which transform the image of the countries and people visited into the self-centred image of the traveller: for as long as things feel strange and a little ridiculous, and the "natives" can be referred to comprehensively as "they," the reader has the sensation of travelling in foreign lands.

To begin with, Leacock speaks from the point

of view of a wide-eyed bucolic whose heart has never seriously left home. He thinks of London, naturally, in terms of South Bend, Indiana. He finds mother-comfort in the thought that the Bank of England acts as agent of the Montana Farmers Trust Company. He is reassured by "the existence of a tall stone monument" in Trafalgar Square because it helps to guide visitors to the two best American barber shops in town. The Tower of London—"the principal penitentiary of the city," where (he gravely adds) "Queen Victoria was imprisoned for many years"—lies due south of the American Garage where "excellent gasoline can be had." The air of optimism that he feels in the streets of London reminds him of the unalloyed confidence that charges the atmosphere of Peterborough, Ontario; and (he is sure) it can only have been impatience to hear the brass band waiting for him in Peterborough that induced the Duke of York, on his last visit to Canada, to decline a warm invitation to leave the train in Orillia and spend an evening with "the boys."

But the narrative thread soon disappears and is developed only slightly in the ninth chapter where he deals with the hazards that beset a public lecturer in Britain. The rest of the sketches explore themes rather than episodes: government, education, the press, capital, prohibition, English humour. Before long the charming and ingenuous rustic has departed and Leacock himself takes control of the action, shaping the landscape to his own vision. We see him change, in the course of five hours of interviewing by the press, from a "dynamo" to an "extinct volcano" and we recognize the Leacock-ian system of accelerated aging. This is a world in which some act of common brutality—an alleged poisoning, for example—can be redeemed by his compassionate sketch of the malefactor: "Miss Mary De Forrest, a handsome brunette thirty-six inches around the hips." In this world, smoking is a mark of swashbuckling manhood and profound thought. Here millionaires, though in this book uncommon, comprise a distinct genus (with species and subspecies) which Leacock observes with fascinated and self-identifying revulsion and attraction. Here a taxi driver can without detectable irony address his fare as "Sir." But by the fourth chapter this fantasy world begins to withdraw and we hear the beguiling but sometimes importunate platform manner of a man confident that his audience will respond at once to his tone, his mannerisms, his public mask, his own infectious enjoyment of his own fun. The voice, rather than the words, becomes the unifying instrument, and we cannot always catch the precise inflection that informs the words with life. Sometimes—being, after all, a professor—he falls into *ex cathedra* opinionism. He looks at Oxford as an educational institution and ends by saying how he thinks women should be educated. He is merry at the expense of the Mother of Parliaments (as who would not be); but when he speaks about business in England, he seems to be expressing, under the clown's immunity, personal desires that would be entirely foreign to Mariposa and unseemly even on Plutoria Avenue.

Light-hearted matter is never far from the tip of Leacock's pen, but the undercurrents are dark. We know what he means about the "gentle and affection-ate ways" of the American customs and immigration officials; and we applaud the editor of *The Times* for his policy of choosing his staff from "men who know" rather than from "men who think"—and making sep-arate arrangements for the thinking. But flashes of a more trenchant irony break the surface of his genial manner like some bitter recollection of a renounced past. The traumatic theme of squalid undergraduate boarding-houses flows back into this book; he notes in passing that the people of England, before they were corrupted by the Americans, were "an honest, law-abiding race, respecting their superiors and despising those below them"; he is sure that if prohibition came to England the benefit would be "intended to fall on the poorer classes" because there is "no desire to inter-fere with the rich." Chapter 7 goes more sombrely than this altogether. Here he argues against "over-exten-sion of government and the decline of individual self-help" and draws a picture of the sprawling octopus of governmental inefficiency clogging "the machinery of bold productive effort." He begins the sketch with some mocking pleasantries about mass unemployment in England and the inflation of the German mark; he ends by urging that the profiteer's rapacity is an essential economic principle, and preaches a lyrical Gospel of Gold based upon "the eager, selfish, and reliant spirit of the man who looks after himself" and "the trained greed of the rascal." Could Leacock, even with his conspiratorial public manner, have made this joke palatable?

My Discovery of England ran through six American printings between June 1922 and January 1923; the Canadian edition was not reissued; the English edition of 1922 was reprinted in 1925 and a cheap edition issued in 1931; in 1924 the whole book was translated into Japanese. There have been no other editions; and although the book includes "Oxford As I See It," Leacock's most frequently reprinted sketch, as a whole it has fallen in the last thirty years or more into a general neglect that at least one of Leacock's foremost recent critics considers undeserved. Certainly Leacock himself is to be clearly seen through the book; and the *Discovery* shows, perhaps more clearly than any other single book of his, the remarkable source from which much of his humour flows: an overflowing and unpredictable fancy, often bizarre, sometimes macabre, that neither exhaustion could disarm nor deliberate effort emasculate. His sense of proportion and disproportion is made equivocal by his own personal uncertainty, yet sharpened by desire and strengthened by compassion. His sense of the grotesque is buoyant and ingenuous enough, we suspect, to make a Siamese execution irrepressibly funny; it might make a delightful because gratuitous fantasy from an ear snipped off (in the manner of Hieronymous Bosch) and mounted between wheels as a chariot for mice to draw in harness. In the *Literary Lapses* there is a classic instance of this sort of vision: in a country barber-shop, we are told, a man is stripped to the waist so that "the barber can then take a rush at him from the other side of the room, and drive the clippers up the full length of the spine, so as to come at the heavier hair on the back of the head with the impact of a lawn-mower driven into long grass." In the *Discovery* the sunnier side of such a gracious vision is represented by the way writers collect impressions from the prone position on the bowsprits of transatlantic vessels; it peeps out from that formidable resting of the brains of Oxford dons between lectures, sometimes for thirty years or more at a time; and unaccountably a female under-graduate (*ancien régime*) sits "for four years as silent as a frog full of shot." A more sinister colour tinges the boarding-house beef that was always "done up in the same way after it was dead." The obsessive grief that paralyses one of Leacock's lecture audiences because of the death (at ninety-four) of the oldest inhabitant is a real sorrow in a real world though Leacock definitely tells us it is not so. The world where, according to the Indian Intelligence in a London newspaper, "two thous-and Parsees had died of the blue plague" and "four thousand agitators had been sentenced to twenty years hard labour each"—with all the foolery about the Shriek of Kowfat—foreshadows, though gaily enough, a world that has now had to accommodate Auschwitz to its memory. His imaginary sketch of England under the blight of Prohibition, though one of the funniest things in the book, is like a communiqué from a twilight city dying of radiation: "We have had the same trouble with wood-alcohol. . . . A great many of our leading actors . . . are dead. And there has been a heavy loss, too, among the literary class and in the legal profession. . . . Some of the best sailors are gone, and it is very difficult to keep admirals." Leacock deplores the English habit of making fun of the prisoners in courts of law. Yet his own story about nearly killing a man with laughter has the impassive horror of nightmare: it is the same sort of joke as those about sailors who break their necks by jumping off ships in cork life-jackets.

Between the ambiguous depths of the dark passages and the infectious swiftness of his gaiety lies the tough and unabashedly singular thread of Stephen Leacock's mind and person. Leacock, not England, stands at the heart of this book. If the book were better unified we should probably know rather less about Leacock than we do; and our knowledge of Leacock's idiosyncrasies, learned from this book alone, heightens our sense of the virtues of his *Discovery of England* and of his distinctive genius altogether.

GEORGE WHALLEY

Queen's University
Kingston, Ontario

THE

BALANCE

OF

TRADE

IN

IMPRESSIONS

For some years past a rising tide of lecturers and literary men from England has washed upon the shores of our North American continent. The purpose of each one of them is to make a new discovery of America. They come over to us travelling in great simplicity, and they return in the ducal suite of the *Aquitania*. They carry away with them their impressions of America, and when they reach England they sell them. This export of impressions has now been going on so long that the balance of trade in impressions is all disturbed. There is no doubt that the Americans and Canadians have been too generous in this matter of giving away impressions. We emit them with the careless ease of a glow-worm, and like the glow-worm ask for nothing in return.

But this irregular and one-sided traffic has now assumed such great proportions that we are compelled to ask whether it is right to allow these people to carry away from us impressions of the very highest commercial value without giving us any pecuniary compensation whatever. British lecturers have been known to land in New York, pass the customs, drive uptown in a closed taxi, and then forward to England *from the closed taxi* itself ten dollars' worth of impressions of American national character. I have myself seen an English literary man—the biggest, I believe: he had at least the appearance of it—sit in the corridor of a fashionable New York hotel and look gloomily into his hat, and then *from his very hat* produce an estimate of the genius of America at twenty cents a word. The nice question as to whose twenty cents that was never seems to have occurred to him.

I am not writing in the faintest spirit of jealousy. I quite admit the extraordinary ability that is involved in this peculiar susceptibility to impressions. I have estimated that some of these English visitors have been able to receive impressions at the rate of four to the second; in fact, they seem to get them every time they see twenty cents. But without jealousy or complaint, I do feel that somehow these impressions are inadequate and fail to depict us as we really are.

Let me illustrate what I mean. Here are some of the impressions of New York, gathered from visitors' discoveries of America and reproduced not perhaps word for word but as closely as I can remember them. "New York," writes one, "nestling at the foot of the Hudson, gave me an impression of cosiness, of tiny graciousness : in short, of weeness." But compare this— "New York," according to another discover of America, "gave me an impression of size, of vastness; there seemed to be a bigness about it not found in smaller places." A third visitor writes, "New York struck me as hard, cruel, almost inhuman." This, I think, was because his taxi driver had charged him three dollars. "The first thing that struck me in New York," writes another, "was the Statue of Liberty." But, after all, that was only natural : it was the first thing that could reach him.

Nor is it only the impressions of the metropolis that seem to fall short of reality. Let me quote a few others taken at random here and there over the continent.

"I took from Pittsburgh," says an English visitor, "an impression of something that I could hardly define—an atmosphere rather than an idea."

All very well. But, after all, had he the right to take it? Granted that Pittsburgh has an atmosphere rather than an idea, the attempt to carry away this atmosphere surely borders on rapacity.

"New Orleans," writes another visitor, "opened her arms to me and bestowed upon me the soft and languorous kiss of the Caribbean." This statement may or may not be true: but in any case it hardly seems the fair thing to mention it.

"Chicago," according to another book of discovery, "struck me as a large city. Situated as it is and where it is, it seems destined to be a place of importance."

Or here, again, is a form of "impression" that recurs again and again—"At Cleveland I felt a distinct note of optimism in the air."

This same note of optimism is found also at Toledo, at Toronto—in short, I believe it indicates nothing more than that someone gave the visitor a cigar. Indeed it generally occurs during the familiar scene in which the visitor describes his cordial reception in an unsuspecting American town: thus:

"I was met at the station (called in America the depot) by a member of the Municipal Council driving his own motor car. After giving me an excellent cigar, he proceeded to drive me about the town, to various points of interest, including the municipal abattoir, where he gave me another excellent cigar, the Carnegie public library, the First National Bank (the courteous manager of which gave me an excellent cigar) and the Second Congregational Church where I had the pleasure of meeting the pastor. The pastor, who appeared a man of breadth and culture, gave me another cigar. In the evening a dinner, admirably cooked and excellently served, was tendered to me at a leading hotel." And of course he took it. After which his statement that he carried away from the town a feeling of optimism explains itself: he had four cigars, the dinner, and half a page of impressions at twenty cents a word.

Nor is it only by the theft of impressions that we suffer at the hands of these English discoverers of America. It is a part of the system also that we have to submit to being lectured to by our talented visitors. It is now quite understood that as soon as an English literary man finishes a book he is rushed across to America to tell the people of the United States and Canada all about it, and how he came to write it. At home, in his own country, they don't care how he came to write it. He's written it and that's enough. But in America it is different. One month after the distinguished author's book on *The Boyhood of Botticelli* has appeared in London, he is seen to land in New York very quietly out of one of the back portholes of the *Olympic*. That same afternoon you will find him in an armchair in one of the big hotels giving off impressions of America to a group of reporters. After which notices appear in all the papers to the effect that he will lecture in Carnegie Hall on *Botticelli the Boy*. The audience is assured beforehand. It consists of all the people who feel that they have to go because they know all about Botticelli and all the people who feel that they have to go because they don't know anything about Botticelli. By this means the lecturer is able to rake the whole country from Montreal to San Francisco with *Botticelli the Boy*. Then he turns round, labels his lecture *Botticelli the Man*, and rakes it all back again. All the way across the continent and back he emits impressions, estimates of national character, and surveys of American genius. He sails from New York in a blaze of publicity, with his cordon of reporters round him, and a month later publishes his book *America As I Saw It*. It is widely read—in America.

In the course of time a very considerable public feeling was aroused in the United States and Canada over this state of affairs. The lack of reciprocity in it seemed unfair. It was felt (or at least I felt) that the time had come when someone ought to go over and take some impressions off England. The choice of such a person (my choice) fell upon myself. By an arrangement with the Geographical Society of America, acting in conjunction with the Royal Geographical Society of England (to both of whom I communicated my proposal), I went at my own expense.

It is scarcely feasible to give here full details in regard to my outfit and equipment, though I hope to do so in a later and more extended account of my expedition. Suffice it to say that my outfit, which was modelled on the equipment of English lecturers in

America, included a complete suit of clothes, a dress shirt for lecturing in, a fountain pen and a silk hat. The dress shirt, I may say for the benefit of other travellers, proved invaluable. The silk hat, however, is no longer used in England except perhaps for scrambling eggs in.

I pass over the details of my pleasant voyage from New York to Liverpool. During the last fifty years so many travellers have made the voyage across the Atlantic that it is now impossible to obtain any impressions from the ocean of the slightest commercial value. My readers will recall the fact that Washington Irving, as far back as a century ago, chronicled the pleasure that one felt during an Atlantic voyage in idle day dreams while lying prone upon the bowsprit and watching the dolphins·leaping in the crystalline foam. Since his time so many gifted writers have attempted to do the same thing that on the large Atlantic liners the bowsprit has been removed, or at any rate a notice put up: "Authors are requested not to lie prostrate on the bowsprit." But even without this advantage, three or four generations of writers have chronicled with great minuteness their sensations during the transit. I need only say that my sensations were just as good as theirs. I will content myself with chronicling the fact that during the voyage we passed two dolphins, one whale and one iceberg (none of them moving very fast at the time), and that on the fourth day out the sea was so rough that the Captain said that in forty years he had never seen such weather. One of the steerage passengers, we were told, was actually washed overboard: I think it was over board that he was washed, but it may have been on board the ship itself.

I pass over also the incidents of my landing in Liverpool, except perhaps to comment upon the extraordinary behaviour of the English customs officials. Without wishing in any way to disturb international relations, one cannot help noticing the rough and inquisitorial methods of the English customs men as compared with the gentle and affectionate ways of the American officials at New York. The two trunks that I brought with me were dragged brutally into an open shed, the strap of one of them was rudely unbuckled, while the lid of the other was actually lifted at least four inches. The trunks were then roughly scrawled with chalk, the lids slammed to, and that was all. Not one of the officials seemed to care to look at my things or to have the politeness to pretend to want to. I had arranged my dress suit and my pajamas so as to make as effective a display as possible : a New York customs officer would have been delighted with it. Here they simply passed it over. "Do open this trunk," I asked one of the officials, "and see my pajamas." "I don't think it is necessary, sir," the man answered. There was a coldness about it that cut me to the quick.

But bad as is the conduct of the English customs men, the immigration officials are even worse. I could not help being struck by the dreadful carelessness with which people are admitted into England. There are, it is true, a group of officials said to be in charge of immigration, but they know nothing of the discriminating care exercised on the other side of the Atlantic.

"Do you want to know," I asked one of them, "whether I am a polygamist?"

"No, sir," he said very quietly.

"Would you like me to tell you whether I am fundamentally opposed to any and every system of government?"

The man seemed mystified. "No, sir," he said. "I don't know that I would."

"Don't you care?" I asked.

"Well, not particularly, sir," he answered.

I was determined to arouse him from his lethargy.

"Let me tell you, then," I said, "that I am an anarchistic polygamist, that I am opposed to all forms of government, that I object to any kind of revealed religion, that I regard the state and property and marriage as the mere tyranny of the bourgeoisie, and that I want to see class hatred carried to the point where it forces everyone into brotherly love. Now, do I get in?"

The official looked puzzled for a minute. "You are not Irish, are you, sir?" he said.

"No."

"Then I think you can come in all right," he answered.

The journey from Liverpool to London, like all other English journeys, is short. This is due to the fact that England is a small country: it contains only 50,000 square miles, whereas the United States, as everyone knows, contains three and a half billion. I mentioned this fact to an English fellow passenger on the train, together with a provisional estimate of the American corn crop for 1922: but he only drew his rug about his knees, took a sip of brandy from his travelling flask, and sank into a state resembling death. I contented myself with jotting down an impression of incivility and paid no further attention to my fellow traveller other than to read the labels on his luggage and to peruse the headings of his newspaper by peeping over his shoulder.

It was my first experience of travelling with a fellow passenger in a compartment of an English train, and I admit now that I was as yet ignorant of the proper method of conduct. Later on I became fully conversant with the rule of travel as understood in England. I should have known, of course, that I must on no account speak to the man. But I should have let down the window a little bit in such as way as to make a strong draught on his ear. Had this failed to break down his reserve I should have placed a heavy valise in the rack over his head so balanced that it might fall on him at any moment. Failing this again, I could have blown rings of smoke at him or stepped on his feet under the pretence of looking out of the window. Under the English rule as long as he bears this in silence you are not supposed to know him. In fact, he is not supposed to be there. You and he each presume the other to be a mere piece of empty space. But let him once be driven to say, "Oh, I beg your pardon, I wonder if you would mind closing the window," and he is lost. After that you are entitled to tell him anything about the corn crop that you care to.

But in the present case I knew nothing of this,

and after three hours of charming silence I found myself in London.

I

AM

INTERVIEWED 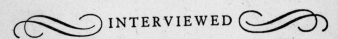 BY

THE PRESS

Immediately upon my arrival in London I was interviewed by the Press. I was interviewed in all twenty times. I am not saying this in any spirit of elation or boastfulness. I am simply stating it as a fact—interviewed twenty times, sixteen times by men and twice by women. But as I feel that the results of these interviews were not all that I could have wished, I think it well to make some public explanation of what happened.

The truth is that we do this thing so differently over in America that I was for the time being completely thrown off my bearings. The questions that I had every right to expect after many years of American and Canadian interviews failed to appear.

28

I pass over the fact that being interviewed for five hours is a fatiguing process. I lay no claim to exemption for that. But to that no doubt was due the singular discrepancies as to my physical appearance which I detected in the London papers.

The young man who interviewed me immediately after breakfast described me as "a brisk, energetic man, still on the right side of forty, with energy in every movement."

The lady who wrote me up at 11.30 reported that my hair was turning grey, and that there was "a peculiar languour" in my manner.

And at the end the boy who took me over at a quarter to two said, "The old gentleman sank wearily upon a chair in the hotel lounge. His hair is almost white."

The trouble is that I had not understood that London reporters are supposed to look at a man's personal appearance. In America we never bother with that. We simply describe him as a "dynamo." For some reason or other it always pleases everybody to be called a "dynamo," and the readers, at least with us, like to read about people who are "dynamos," and hardly care for anything else.

In the case of very old men we sometimes call them "battle horses" or "extinct volcanoes," but beyond these three classes we hardly venture on description. So I was misled. I had expected that the reporter would say: "As soon as Mr Leacock came across the floor we felt we were in the presence of a 'dynamo' (or an 'extinct battle horse' as the case may be)." Otherwise I would have kept up those energetic movements all the morning. But they fatigue me, and I did not think them necessary. But I let that pass.

The more serious trouble was the questions put to me by the reporters. Over in our chief centres of population we use another set altogether. I am thinking here especially of the kind of interview that I have given out in Youngstown, Ohio, and Richmond, Indiana, and Peterborough, Ontario. In all these places—for example, in Youngstown, Ohio—the reporter asks as his first question, "What is your impression of Youngstown?"

In London they don't. They seem indifferent to the fate of their city. Perhaps it is only English pride. For all I know they may have been burning to know this, just as the Youngstown, Ohio, people are, and were too proud to ask. In any case I will insert here the answer I had written out in my pocketbook (one copy for each paper—the way we do it in Youngstown), and which read:

"London strikes me as emphatically a city with a future. Standing as she does in the heart of a rich agricultural district with railroad connection in all directions, and resting, as she must, on a bed of coal and oil, I prophesy that she will one day be a great city."

The advantage of this is that it enables the reporter to get just the right kind of heading: PROPHESIES BRIGHT FUTURE FOR LONDON. Had that been used my name would have stood higher there than it does today —unless the London people are very different from the people in Youngstown, which I doubt. As it is they don't know whether their future is bright or is as dark as mud. But it's not my fault. The reporters never asked me.

If the first question had been handled properly it would have led up by an easy and pleasant transition to question two, which always runs: "Have you seen our factories?" To which the answer is:

"I have. I was taken out early this morning by a group of your citizens (whom I cannot thank enough) in a Ford car to look at your pail and bucket works. At eleven-thirty I was taken out by a second group in what was apparently the same car to see your soap works. I understand that you are the second nail-making centre east of the Alleghenies, and I am amazed and appalled.

This afternoon I am to be taken out to see your wonderful system of disposing of sewerage, a thing which has fascinated me from childhood."

Now I am not offering any criticism of the London system of interviewing, but one sees at once how easy and friendly for all concerned this Youngstown method is; how much better it works than the London method of asking questions about literature and art and difficult things of that sort. I am sure that there must be soap works and perhaps a pail factory somewhere in London. But during my entire time of residence there no one ever offered to take me to them. As for the sewerage—oh, well, I suppose we are more hospitable in America. Let it go at that.

I had my answer all written and ready, saying:

"I understand that London is the second greatest hop-consuming, the fourth hog-killing, and the first egg-absorbing centre in the world."

But what I deplore still more, and I think with reason, is the total omission of the familiar interrogation: "What is your impression of our women?"

That's where the reporter over on our side hits the nail every time. That is the point at which we always nudge him in the ribs and buy him a cigar, and at which youth and age join in a sly jest together. Here again the sub-heading comes in so nicely: THINKS YOUNGSTOWN WOMEN CHARMING. And they are. They are, everywhere. But I hate to think that I had to keep my impression of London women unused in my pocket while a young man asked me whether I thought modern literature owed more to observation and less to inspiration than some other kind of literature.

Now that's exactly the kind of question, the last one, that the London reporters seem to harp on. They seem hipped about literature; and their questions are too difficult. One asked me whether the American drama was structurally inferior to the French. I don't call that fair. I told him I didn't know; that I used to know the answer to it when I was at college, but that I had forgotten it, and that, anyway, I am too well off now to need to remember it.

That question is only one of a long list that they asked me about art and literature. I missed nearly all of them, except one as to whether I thought Al Jolson or Frank Tinney was the higher artist, and even that one was asked by an American who is wasting himself on the London Press.

I don't want to speak in anger. But I say it frankly, the atmosphere of these young men is not healthy, and I felt that I didn't want to see them any more.

Had there been a reporter of the kind we have at home in Montreal or Toledo or Springfield, Illinois, I would have welcomed him at my hotel. He could have taken me out in a Ford car and shown me a factory and told me how many cubic feet of water go down the Thames in an hour. I should have been glad of his society, and he and I would have together made up the kind of copy that people of his class and mine read. But I felt that if any young man came along to ask about the structure of the modern drama, he had better go to the British Museum.

Meantime as the reporters entirely failed to elicit the large fund of information which I acquired, I reserve my impressions of London for a chapter by themselves.

IMPRESSIONS

OF

LONDON

Before setting down my impressions of the great English metropolis—a phrase which I have thought out as a designation for London—I think it proper to offer an initial apology. I find that I receive impressions with great difficulty and have nothing of that easy facility in picking them up which is shown by British writers on America. I remember Hugh Walpole telling me that he could hardly walk down Broadway without getting at least three dollars' worth and on Fifth Avenue five dollars' worth; and I recollect that St John Ervine came up to my house in Montreal, drank a cup of tea, borrowed some tobacco, and got away with sixty dollars' worth of impressions of Canadian life and character.

For this kind of thing I have only a despairing

admiration. I can get an impression if I am given time and can think about it beforehand. But it requires thought. The fact was all the more distressing to me in as much as one of the leading editors of America had made me a proposal, as honourable to him as it was lucrative to me, that immediately on my arrival in London—or just before it—I should send him a thousand words on the genius of the English, and five hundred words on the spirit of London, and two hundred words of personal chat with Lord Northcliffe. This contract I was unable to fulfil except the personal chat with Lord Northcliffe, which proved an easy matter as he happened to be away in Australia.

But I have since pieced together my impressions as conscientiously as I could and I present them here. If they seem to be a little bit modelled on British impressions of America I admit at once that the influence is there. We writers all act and react on one another; and when I see a good thing in another man's book I react on it at once.

London, the name of which is already known to millions of readers of this book, is beautifully situated on the river Thames, which here sweeps in a wide curve with much the same breadth and majesty as the St Jo River at South Bend, Indiana. London, like South Bend itself, is a city of clean streets and admirable sidewalks, and has an excellent water supply. One is at once struck by the number of excellent and well appointed motor cars that one sees on every hand, the neatness of the shops and the cleanliness and cheerfulness of the faces of the people. In short, as an English visitor said of Peterborough, Ontario, there is a distinct note of optimism in the air. I forget who it was who said this, but at any rate I have been in Peterborough myself and I have seen it.

Contrary to my expectations and contrary to all our transatlantic precedents, I was *not* met at the depot by one of the leading citizens, himself a member of the Municipal Council, driving his own motor car. He did *not* tuck a fur rug about my knees, present me with a really excellent cigar and proceed to drive me about the town so as to show me the leading points of interest, the municipal reservoir, the gas works and the municipal abattoir. In fact he was not there. But I attribute his absence not to any lack of hospitality but merely to a certain reserve in the English character.

They are as yet unused to the arrival of lecturers. When they get to be more accustomed to their coming, they will learn to take them straight to the municipal abattoir just as we do.

For lack of better guidance, therefore, I had to form my impressions of London by myself. In the mere physical sense there is much to attract the eye. The city is able to boast of many handsome public buildings and offices which compare favourably with anything on the other side of the Atlantic. On the bank of the Thames itself rises the power house of the Westminster Electric Supply Corporation, a handsome modern edifice in the later Japanese style. Close by are the commodious premises of the Imperial Tobacco Company, while at no great distance the Chelsea Gas Works add a striking feature of rotundity. Passing northward, one observes Westminster Bridge, notable as a principal station of the underground railway. This station and the one next above it, the Charing Cross one, are connected by a wide thoroughfare called Whitehall. One of the best American drug stores is here situated. The upper end of Whitehall opens into the majestic and spacious Trafalgar Square. Here are grouped in imposing proximity the offices of the Canadian Pacific and other railways, the International Sleeping Car Company, the Montreal *Star*, and the Anglo-Dutch Bank. Two of the best American barber shops are conveniently grouped near the Square, while the existence of a tall stone monument in the middle of the Square itself enables the American visitor to find them without difficulty. Passing eastward towards the heart of the city, one notes on the left hand the imposing pile of St Paul's, an enormous church with a round dome on the top, suggesting strongly the First Church of Christ (Scientist) on Euclid Avenue, Cleveland. But the English churches not being labelled, the visitor is often at a loss to distinguish them.

A little further on one finds oneself in the heart of financial London. Here all the great financial institutions of America—the First National Bank of Milwaukee, the Planters National Bank of St Louis, the Montana Farmers Trust Co., and many others—have either their offices or their agents. The Bank of England —which acts as the London agent of the Montana Farmers Trust Company—and the London County Bank, which represents the People's Deposit Co., of Yonkers, N. Y., are said to be in the neighbourhood.

This particular part of London is connected with the existence of that strange and mysterious thing called "the City." I am still unable to decide whether the City is a person, or a place, or a thing. But as a form of being I give it credit for being the most emotional, the most volatile, the most peculiar creature in the world. You read in the morning paper that the City is "deeply depressed." At noon it is reported that the City is "buoyant" and by four o'clock the City is "wildly excited."

I have tried in vain to find the causes of these peculiar changes of feeling. The ostensible reasons, as given in the newspaper, are so trivial as to be hardly worthy of belief. For example, here is the kind of news that comes out from the City. "The news that a *modus vivendi* has been signed between the Sultan of Kowfat and the Shriek-ul-Islam has caused a sudden buoyancy in the City. Steel rails which had been depressed all morning reacted immediately while American mules rose up sharply to par." . . . "Monsieur Poincaré, speaking at Bordeaux, said that henceforth France must seek to retain by all possible means the ping-pong championship of the world : values in the City collapsed at once." . . . "Despatches from Bombay say that the Shah of Persia yesterday handed a golden slipper to the Grand Vizier Feebli Pasha as a sign that he might go and chase himself : the news was at once followed by a drop in oil, and a rapid attempt to liquidate everything that is fluid. . . ."

But these mysteries of the City I do not pretend to explain. I have passed through the place dozens of times and never noticed anything particular in the way of depression or buoyancy, or falling oil, or rising rails. But no doubt it is there.

A little beyond the City and further down the river the visitor finds this district of London terminating in the gloomy and forbidding Tower, the principal penitentiary of the city. Here Queen Victoria was imprisoned for many years.

Excellent gasoline can be had at the American Garage immediately north of the Tower, where motor repairs of all kinds are also carried on.

These, however, are but the superficial pictures of London, gathered by the eye of the tourist. A far deeper meaning is found in the examination of the great historic monuments of the city. The principal ones of these are the Tower of London (just mentioned), the

British Museum and Westminster Abbey. No visitor to London should fail to see these. Indeed he ought to feel that his visit to England is wasted unless he has seen them. I speak strongly on the point because I feel strongly on it. To my mind there is something about the grim fascination of the historic Tower, the cloistered quiet of the Museum and the majesty of the ancient Abbey, which will make it the regret of my life that I didn't see any one of the three. I fully meant to: but I failed: and I can only hope that the circumstances of my failure may be helpful to other visitors.

The Tower of London I most certainly intended to inspect. Each day, after the fashion of every tourist, I wrote for myself a little list of things to do and I always put the Tower of London on it. No doubt the reader knows the kind of little list I mean. It runs:

1 Go to bank
2 Buy a shirt
3 National Picture Gallery
4 Razor blades
5 Tower of London
6 Soap

This itinerary, I regret to say, was never carried out in full. I was able at times both to go to the bank and buy a shirt in a single morning: at other times I was able to buy razor blades and almost to find the National Picture Gallery. Meantime I was urged on all sides by my London acquaintances not to fail to see the Tower. "There's a grim fascination about the place," they said; "you mustn't miss it." I am quite certain that in due course of time I should have made my way to the Tower but for the fact that I made a fatal discovery. I found out that the London people who urged me to go and see the Tower had never seen it themselves. It appears they never go near it. One night at a dinner a man next to me said, "Have you seen the Tower? You really ought to. There's a grim fascination about it." I looked him in the face. "Have you seen it yourself?" I asked. "Oh, yes," he answered. "I've seen it." "When?" I asked. The man hesitated. "When I was just a boy," he said, "my father took me there." "How long ago is that?" I inquired. "About forty years ago," he answered. "I always mean to go again but I don't somehow seem to get the time."

After this I got to understand that when a Londoner says, "Have you seen the Tower of London?" the answer is "No, and neither have you."

Take the parallel case of the British Museum. Here is a place that is a veritable treasure house. A repository of some of the most priceless historical relics to be found upon the earth. It contains, for instance, the famous Papyrus Manuscript of Thotmes II of the first Egyptian dynasty—a thing known to scholars all over the world as the oldest extant specimen of what can be called writing; indeed one can here see the actual evolution (I am quoting from a work of reference, or at least from my recollection of it) from the ideographic cuneiform of the phonetic syllabic script. Every time I have read about that manuscript and have happened to be in Orillia (Ontario) or Schenectady (N. Y.) or any such place, I have felt that I would be willing to take a whole trip to England to have five minutes at the British

Museum, just five, to look at that papyrus. Yet as soon as I got to London this changed. The railway stations of London have been so arranged that to get to any train for the north or west, the traveller must pass the British Museum. The first time I went by it in a taxi, I felt quite a thrill. "Inside those walls," I thought to myself, "is the manuscript of Thotmes II." The next time I actually stopped the taxi. "Is that the British Museum?" I asked the driver. "I think it is something of the sort, sir," he said. I hesitated. "Drive me," I said, "to where I can buy safety razor blades."

After that I was able to drive past the Museum with the quiet assurance of a Londoner, and to take part in dinner table discussions as to whether the British Museum or the Louvre contains the greater treasures. It is quite easy any way. All you have to do is to remember that the Winged Victory of Samothrace is in the Louvre and the papyrus of Thotmes II (or some such document) is in the Museum.

The Abbey, I admit, is indeed majestic. I did not intend to miss going into it. But I felt, as so many tourists have, that I wanted to enter it in the proper frame of mind. I never got into the frame of mind; at least not when near the Abbey itself. I have been in exactly that frame of mind when on State Street, Chicago, or on King Street, Toronto, or anywhere three thousand miles away from the Abbey. But by bad luck I never struck both the frame of mind and the Abbey at the same time.

But the Londoners, after all, in not seeing their own wonders, are only like the rest of the world. The people who live in Buffalo never go to see Niagara Falls; people in Cleveland don't know which is Mr Rockefeller's house, and people live and even die in New York without going up to the top of the Woolworth Building. And anyway the past is remote and the present is near. I know a cab driver in the city of Quebec whose business in life it is to drive people up to see the Plains of Abraham, but unless they bother him to do it, he doesn't even show them the spot where Wolfe fell: what he does point out with real zest is the place where the Mayor and the City Council sat on the wooden platform that they put up for the municipal celebration last summer.

No description of London would be complete without a reference, however brief, to the singular salubrity and charm of the London climate. This is seen at its best during the autumn and winter months. The climate of London and indeed of England generally is due to the influence of the Gulf Stream. The way it works is thus: The Gulf Stream, as it nears the shores of the British Isles and feels the propinquity of Ireland, rises into the air, turns into soup, and comes down on London. At times the soup is thin and is in fact little more than a mist: at other times it has the consistency of a thick Potage St Germain. London people are a little sensitive on the point and flatter their atmosphere by calling it a fog: but it is not: it is soup. The notion that no sunlight ever gets through and that in the London winter people never see the sun is of course a ridiculous error, circulated no doubt by the jealousy of foreign nations. I have myself seen the sun plainly visible in London, without the aid of glasses, on a November day in broad daylight; and again one night about four o'clock in the afternoon I saw the sun distinctly appear through the clouds. The whole subject of daylight in the London winter is, however, one which belongs rather to the technique of astronomy than to a book of description. In practice daylight is but little used. Electric lights are burned all the time in all houses, buildings, railway stations and clubs. This practice which is now universally observed is called Daylight Saving.

But the distinction between day and night during the London winter is still quite obvious to any one of an observant mind. It is indicated by various signs such as the striking of clocks, the tolling of bells, the closing of saloons, and the raising of taxi rates. It is much less easy to distinguish the technical approach of night in the other cities of England that lie outside the confines, physical and intellectual, of London and live in a continuous gloom. In such places as the great manufacturing cities, Buggingham-under-Smoke, or Gloomsbury-on-Ooze, night may be said to be perpetual.

I had written the whole of the above chapter and looked on it as finished when I realized that I had made a terrible omission. I neglected to say anything about the Mind of London. This is a thing that is always put into any book of discovery and observation and I can only apologize for not having discussed it sooner. I am quite familiar with other people's chapters on "The

Mind of America," and "The Chinese Mind," and so forth. Indeed, so far as I know it has turned out that almost everybody all over the world has a mind. Nobody nowadays travels, even in Central America or Tibet, without bringing back a chapter on "The Mind of Costa Rica," or on the "Psychology of the Mongolian." Even the gentler peoples such as the Burmese, the Siamese, the Hawaiians, and the Russians, though they have no minds are written up as souls.

It is quite obvious then that there is such a thing as the mind of London: and it is all the more culpable in me to have neglected it in as much as my editorial friend in New York had expressly mentioned it to me before I sailed. "What," said he, leaning far over his desk after his massive fashion and reaching out into the air, "what is in the *minds* of these people? Are they," he added, half to himself, though I heard him, "are they thinking? And, if they think, *what* do they think?"

I did therefore, during my stay in London, make an accurate study of the things that London seemed to be thinking about. As a comparative basis for this study I brought with me a carefully selected list of the things that New York was thinking about at the moment. These I selected from the current newspapers in the proportions to the amount of space allotted to each topic and the size of the heading that announced it. Having thus a working idea of what I may call the mind of New York, I was able to collect and set beside it a list of similar topics, taken from the London Press to represent the mind of London. The two placed side by side make an interesting piece of psychological analysis. They read as follows:

THE MIND OF NEW YORK	THE MIND OF LONDON
What is it thinking?	*What is it thinking?*
1 Do chorus girls make good wives?	1 Do chorus girls marry well?
2 Is red hair a sign of temperament?	2 What is red hair a sign of?
3 Can a woman be in love with two men?	3 Can a man be in love with two women?
4 Is fat a sign of genius?	4 Is genius a sign of fat?

Looking over these lists, I think it is better to present them without comment; I feel sure that somewhere or other in them one should detect the heart throbs, the pulsations of two great peoples. But I don't get it. In fact the two lists look to me terribly like "the mind of Costa Rica."

The same editor also advised me to mingle, at his expense, in the brilliant intellectual life of England. "There," he said, "is a coterie of men, probably the most brilliant group east of the Mississippi." (I think he said the Mississippi.) "You will find them," he said to me, "brilliant, witty, filled with repartee." He suggested that I should send him back, as far as words could express it, some of this brilliance. I was very glad to be able to do this, although I fear that the results were not at all what he had anticipated. Still, I held conversations with these people and I gave him, in all truthfulness the result. Sir James Barrie said, "This is really very exceptional weather for this time of year." Cyril Maude said, "And so a Martini cocktail is merely gin and vermouth." Ian Hay said, "You'll find the underground ever so handy once you understand it."

I have a lot more of these repartees that I could insert here if it was necessary. But somehow I feel that it is not.

A

CLEAR

VIEW

OF
THE GOVERNMENT
AND
POLITICS OF ENGLAND

A loyal British subject like myself in dealing with the government of England should necessarily begin with a discussion of the monarchy. I have never had the pleasure of meeting the King except once on the G.T.R. platform in Orillia, Ontario, when he was the Duke of York and I was one of the welcoming delegates of the town council. No doubt he would recall it in a minute.

But in England the King is surrounded by formality and circumstance. On many mornings I waited round the gates of Buckingham Palace but I found it quite impossible to meet the King in the quiet sociable way in which one met him in Orillia. The English, it seems, love to make the kingship a subject of great pomp and official etiquette. In Canada it is quite different. Perhaps we understand kings and princes better than the English do. At any rate we treat them in a far more human heart-to-heart fashion than is the English custom, and they respond to it at once. I remember when King George—he was, as I say, Duke of York then—came up to Orillia, Ontario, how we all met him in a delegation on the platform. Bob Curran—Bob was Mayor of the town that year—went up to him and shook hands with him and invited him to come right on up to Orillia House where he had a room reserved for him. Charlie Janes and Mel Tudhope and the other boys who were on the town council gathered round the royal prince and shook hands and told him that he simply must stay over. George Rapley, the bank manager, said that if he wanted a cheque cashed or anything of that sort to come right into the Royal Bank and he would do it for him. The prince had two aides-de-camp with him and a secretary, but Bob Curran said to bring them uptown too and it would be all right. We had planned to have an oyster supper for the Prince at Jim Smith's hotel and then take him either to the Y.M.C.A. Pool Room or else to the tea social in the basement of the Presbyterian Church.

Unluckily the prince couldn't stay. It turned out that he had to get right back into his train and go on to Peterborough, Ontario, where they were to have a brass band to meet him, which naturally he didn't want to miss.

But the point is that it was a real welcome. And you could see that the prince appreciated it. There was a warmth and a meaning to it that the prince understood at once. It was a pity that he couldn't have stayed over and had time to see the carriage factory and the new sewerage plant. We all told the prince that he must come back and he said that if he could he most certainly would. When the prince's train pulled out of the station and we all went back uptown together (it was before prohibition came to Ontario) you could feel that the institution of royalty was quite solid in Orillia for a generation.

But you don't get that sort of thing in England. There's a formality and coldness in all their dealings with royalty that would never go down with us. They like to have the King come and open Parliament dressed in royal robes, and with a clattering troop of soldiers

54

riding in front of him. As for taking him over to the Y.M.C.A. to play pin pool, they never think of it. They have seen so much of the mere *outside* of his kingship that they don't understand the *heart* of it as we do in Canada.

But let us turn to the House of Commons: for no description of England would be complete without at least some mention of this interesting body. Indeed for the ordinary visitor to London the greatest interest of all attaches to the spacious and magnificent Parliament Buildings. The House of Commons is commodiously situated beside the River Thames. The principal features of the House are the large lunch room on the western side and the tea-room on the terrace on the eastern. A series of smaller luncheon rooms extend (apparently) all round about the premises: while a commodious bar offers a ready access to the members at all hours of the day. While any members are in the bar a light is kept burning in the tall Clock Tower at one corner of the building, but when the bar is closed the light is turned off by whichever of the Scotch members leaves last. There is a handsome legislative chamber attached to the premises from which—so the antiquarians tell us—the House of Commons took its name. But it is not usual now for the members to sit in the legislative chamber as the legislation is now all done outside, either at the home of Mr Lloyd George, or at the National Liberal Club, or at one or other of the newspaper offices. The House, however, is called together at very frequent intervals to give it an opportunity of hearing the latest legislation and allowing the members to indulge in cheers, sighs, groans, votes and other expressions of vitality. After having cheered as much as is good for it, it goes back again to the lunch rooms and goes on eating till needed again.

It is, however, an entire exaggeration to say that the House of Commons no longer has a real share in the government of England. This is not so. Anybody connected with the government values House of Commons in a high degree. One of the leading newspaper proprietors of London himself told me that he has always felt that if he had the House of Commons on his side he had a very valuable ally. Many of the labour leaders are inclined to regard the House of Commons as of great utility, while the leading women's organizations, now that women are admitted as members, may be said to regard the House as one of themselves.

Looking around to find just where the natural service of the House of Commons comes in, I am inclined to think that it must be in the practice of "asking questions" in the House. Whenever anything goes wrong a member rises and asks a question. He gets up, for example, with a little paper in his hand, and asks the government if ministers are aware that the Khedive of Egypt was seen yesterday wearing a Turkish Tarbosh. Ministers say very humbly that they hadn't known it, and a thrill runs through the whole country. The members can apparently ask any questions they like. In the repeated visits which I made to the gallery of the House of Commons I was unable to find any particular sense or meaning in the questions asked, though no doubt they had an intimate bearing on English politics not clear to an outsider like myself. I heard one member ask the government whether they were aware that herrings were being imported from Hamburg to Harwich. The government said no. Another member rose and asked the government whether they considered Shakespeare or Molière the greatest dramatic artist. The government answered that ministers were taking this under their earnest consideration and that a report would be submitted to Parliament. Another member asked the government if they knew who won the Queen's Plate this season at Toronto. They did—in fact this member got in wrong, as this is the very thing that the government do know. Towards the close of the evening a member rose and asked the government if they knew what time it was. The Speaker, however, ruled this question out of order on the ground that it had been answered before.

The Parliament Buildings are so vast that it is not possible to state with certainty what they do, or do not, contain. But it is generally said that somewhere in the building is the House of Lords. When they meet they are said to come together very quietly shortly before the dinner hour, take a glass of dry sherry and a biscuit (they are all abstemious men), reject whatever bills may be before them at the moment, take another dry sherry and then adjourn for two years.

The public are no longer allowed unrestricted access to the Houses of Parliament; its approaches are now strictly guarded by policemen. In order to obtain admission it is necessary either to (A) communicate in writing with the Speaker of the House, enclosing certificates of naturalization and proof of identity, or (B) give the policeman five shillings. Method B is the one usually adopted. On great nights, however, when the House of Commons is sitting and is about to do something important, such as ratifying a Home Rule Bill or cheering, or welcoming a new lady member, it is not possible to enter by merely bribing the policeman with five shillings; it takes a pound. The English people complain bitterly of the rich Americans who have in this way corrupted the London public. Before they were corrupted they would do anything for sixpence.

This peculiar vein of corruption by the Americans runs like a thread, I may say, through all the texture of English life. Among those who have been principally exposed to it are the servants—especially butlers and chauffeurs, hotel porters, bellboys, railway porters and guards, all taxi drivers, pew openers, curates, bishops, and a large part of the peerage.

The terrible ravages that have been made by the Americans on English morality are witnessed on every hand. Whole classes of society are hopelessly damaged. I have it in the evidence of the English themselves and there seems to be no doubt of the fact. Till the Americans came to England the people were an honest, law-abiding race, respecting their superiors and despising those below them. They had never been corrupted by money and their employers extended to them in this regard their tenderest solicitude. Then the Americans came. Servants ceased to be what they were; butlers were hopelessly damaged; hotel porters became a wreck; taxi drivers turned out thieves; curates could no longer be trusted to handle money; peers sold their daughters at a million dollars a piece or three for two. In fact the whole kingdom began to deteriorate till it got where it is now. At present after a rich American has stayed in any English country house, its owners find that they can do nothing with the butler; a wildness has come over the man. There is a restlessness in his demeanour and a strange wistful look in his eye as if seeking for something. In many cases, so I understand, after an American has stayed in a country house, the butler goes insane. He is found in his pantry counting over the sixpence given to him by a Duke, and laughing to himself. He has to be taken in charge by the police. With him generally go the chauffeur, whose mind has broken down from driving a rich American twenty miles; and the gardener, who is found tearing up raspberry bushes by the roots to see if there is any money under them; and the local curate whose brain has collapsed or expanded, I forget which, when a rich American gave him fifty dollars for his soup kitchen.

There are, it is true, a few classes that have escaped this contagion, shepherds living in the hills, drovers, sailors, fishermen and such like. I remember the first time I went into the English countryside being struck with the clean, honest look in the people's faces. I realized exactly where they got it: they had never seen any Americans. I remember speaking to an aged peasant down in Somerset. "Have you ever seen any Americans?" "Nah," he said, "uz eeard a mowt o' 'em, zir, but uz zeen nowt o' 'em." It was clear that the noble fellow was quite undamaged by American contact.

Now the odd thing about this corruption is

that exactly the same idea is held on the other side of the water. It is a known fact that if a young English Lord comes to an American town he puts it to the bad in one week. Socially the whole place goes to pieces. Girls whose parents are in the hardware business and who used to call their father "Pop" begin to talk of precedence and whether a Duchess Dowager goes in to dinner ahead of or behind a countess scavenger. After the young Lord has attended two dances and one tea-social in the Methodist Church Sunday School Building (Adults 25 cents, children 10 cents—all welcome) there is nothing for the young men of the town to do except to drive him out or go further west.

One can hardly wonder then that this general corruption has extended even to the policemen who guard the Houses of Parliament. On the other hand this vein of corruption has not extended to English politics. Unlike ours, English politics—one hears it on every hand—are pure. Ours unfortunately are known to be not so. The difference seems to be that our politicians will do anything for money and the English politicians won't; they just take the money and won't do a thing for it.

Somehow there always seems to be a peculiar interest about English political questions that we don't find elsewhere. At home in Canada our politics turn on such things as how much money the Canadian National Railways lose as compared with how much they could lose if they really tried; on whether the Grain Growers of Manitoba should be allowed to import ploughs without paying a duty or to pay a duty without importing the ploughs. Our members at Ottawa discuss such things as highway subsidies, dry farming, the Bank Act, and the tariff on hardware. These things leave me absolutely cold. To be quite candid there is something terribly plebeian about them. In short, our politics are what we call in French *"peuple."*

But when one turns to England, what a striking difference! The English, with the whole huge British Empire to fish in and the European system to draw upon, can always dig up some kind of political topic of discussion that has a real charm about it. One month you find English politics turning on the Oasis of Merv and the next on the hinterland of Albania; or a member rises in the Commons with a little bit of paper in his hand and desires to ask the foreign secretary if he is aware that the Ahkoond of Swat is dead. The foreign secretary states that the government have no information other than that the Ahkoond *was* dead a month ago. There is a distinct sensation in the House at the realisation that the Akhoond has been dead a month without the House having known that he was alive. The sensation is conveyed to the Press and the afternoon papers appear with large headings, THE AHKOOND OF SWAT IS DEAD. The public who have never heard of the Ahkoond bare their heads in a moment in a pause to pray for the Ahkoond's soul. Then the cables take up the refrain and word is flashed all over the world, THE AKHOOND OF SWAT IS DEAD.

There was a Canadian journalist and poet once who was so impressed with the news that the Akhoond was dead, so bowed down with regret that he had never known the Akhoond while alive, that he forthwith wrote a poem in memory of *The Akhoond of Swat*. I have always thought that the reason for the wide admiration that Lannigan's verses received was not merely because of the brilliant wit that is in them but because in a wider sense they typify so beautifully the scope of English politics. The death of the Ahkoond of Swat, and whether Great Britain should support as his successor Mustalpha El Djin or Kamu Flaj—there is something worth talking of over an afternoon tea table. But suppose that the whole of the Manitoba Grain Growers were to die. What could one say about it? They'd be dead, that's all.

So it is that people all over the world turn to English politics with interest. What more delightful than to open an atlas, find out where the new kingdom of Hejaz is, and then violently support the British claim to a protectorate over it. Over in America we don't understand this sort of thing. There is naturally little chance to do so and we don't know how to use it when it comes. I remember that when a chance did come in connection with the great Venezuela dispute over the ownership of the jungles and mud flats of British Guiana, the American papers at once inserted headings, WHERE IS THE ESSIQUIBO RIVER? That spoiled the whole thing. If you admit that you don't know where a place is, then the bottom is knocked out of all discussion. But if you pretend that you do, then you are all right. Mr Lloyd George is said to have caused great amusement at the Versailles Conference by admitting that he hadn't known where Teschen was. So at least it was reported in the papers; and for all I know it might even have been true. But the fun that he raised was not really half what could have been raised. I have it on good authority that two of the American delegates hadn't known where Austria Proper was and thought that Unredeemed Italy was on the East Side of New York, while the Chinese delegate thought that the Cameroons were part of Scotland. But it is these little geographic niceties that lend a charm to European politics that ours lack forever.

I don't mean to say the English politics always turn on romantic places or on small questions. They don't. They often include questions of the largest order. But when the English introduce a really large question as the basis of their politics they like to select one that is insoluble. This guarantees that it will last. Take for example the rights of the Crown as against the people. That lasted for one hundred years—all the seventeenth century. In Oklahoma or in Alberta they would have called a convention on the question, settled it in two weeks and spoiled it for further use. In the same way the Protestant Reformation was used for a hundred years and the Reform Bill for a generation.

At the present time the genius of the English for politics has selected as their insoluble political question the topic of the German indemnity. The essence of the problem as I understand it may be stated as follows:

It was definitely settled by the Conference at Versailles that Germany is to pay the Allies 3,912,486,782,421 marks. I think that is the correct figure, though of course I am speaking only from memory. At any rate, the correct figure is within a hundred billion marks of the above.

The sum to be paid was not reached without a great deal of discussion. Monsieur Briand, the French Minister, is reported to have thrown out the figure 4,281,390,687,471. But Mr Lloyd George would not pick it up. Nor do I blame him unless he had a basket to pick it up with.

Lloyd George's point of view was that the Germans could very properly pay a limited amount such as 3,912,486,782,421 marks, but it was not feasible to put on them a burden of 4,281,390,687,471 marks.

By the way if any one at this point doubts the accuracy of the figures just given, all he has to do is to take the amount of the indemnity as stated in gold marks and then multiply it by the present value of the mark and he will find to his chagrin that the figures are correct. If he is still not satisfied I refer him to a book of logarithms. If he is not satisfied with that I refer him to any work on conic sections and if not convinced even then I refer him so far that he will never come back.

The indemnity being thus fixed, the next question is as to the method of collecting it. In the first place there is no intention of allowing the Germans to pay in actual cash. If they do this they will merely inflate the English beyond what is bearable. England has been inflated now for eight years and has had enough of it.

In the second place, it is understood that it will not do to allow the Germans to offer 4,281,390,687,471 marks' worth of coal. It is more than the country needs.

What is more, if the English want coal they propose to buy it in an ordinary decent way from a Christian coal dealer in their own country. They do not purpose to ruin their own coal industry for the sake of building up the prosperity of the German nation.

What I say of coal is applied with equal force to any offers of food, grain, oil, petroleum, gas, or any other natural product. Payment in any of these will be sternly refused. Even now it is all the British farmers can do to live and for some it is more. Many of them are having to sell off their motors and pianos and to send their sons to college to work. At the same time, the German producer by depressing the mark further and further is able to work fourteen hours a day. This argument may not be quite correct but I take it as I find it in the London Press. Whether I state it correctly or not, it is quite plain that the problem is insoluble. That is all that is needed in first-class politics.

A really good question like the German reparation question will go on for a century. Undoubtedly in the year 2000 A.D., a British Chancellor of the Exchequer will still be explaining that the government is fully resolved that Germany shall pay to the last farthing (*cheers*): but that ministers have no intention of allowing the German payment to take a form that will undermine British industry (*wild applause*): that the German indemnity shall be so paid that without weakening the power of the Germans to buy from us it shall increase our power of selling to them.

Such questions last for ever.

On the other hand sometimes by sheer carelessness a question gets settled and passes out of politics. This, so we are given to understand, has happened to the Irish question. It is settled. A group of Irish delegates and British ministers got together round a table and settled it. The settlement has since been celebrated at a demonstration of brotherhood by the Irish Americans of New York with only six casualties. Henceforth the Irish question passes into history. There may be some odd fighting along the Ulster border, or a little civil war with perhaps a little revolution every now and then, but as a question the thing is finished.

I must say that I for one am very sorry to think that the Irish question is gone. We shall miss it greatly. Debating societies which have flourished on it ever since 1886 will be wrecked for want of it. Dinner parties will now lose half the sparkle of their conversation. It will be no longer possible to make use of such good old remarks as "After all the Irish are a gifted people," or "You must remember that fifty per cent of the great English generals were Irish."

The settlement turned out to be a very simple affair. Ireland was merely given dominion status. What that is, no one knows, but it means that the Irish have now got it, and that they sink from the high place that they had in the white light of publicity to the level of the Canadians or the New Zealanders.

Whether it is quite a proper thing to settle trouble by conferring dominion status on it, is open to question. It is a practice that is bound to spread. It is rumoured that it is now contemplated to confer dominion status upon the Borough of Poplar and on the Cambridge undergraduates. It is even understood that at the recent disarmament conference England offered to confer dominion status on the United States. President Harding would assuredly have accepted it at once but for the protest of Mr Briand, who claimed that any such offer must be accompanied by a permission to increase the French fire-brigade by fifty per cent.

It is lamentable, too, that at the very same moment when the Irish question was extinguished, the Naval Question which had lasted for nearly fifty years was absolutely obliterated by disarmament. Henceforth the alarm of invasion is a thing of the past and the navy practically needless. Beyond keeping a fleet in the North Sea and one in the Mediterranean, and maintaining a patrol all round the rim of the Pacific Ocean, Britain will cease to be a naval power. A mere annual expenditure of fifty million pounds sterling will suffice for such thin pretence of naval preparedness as a disarmed nation will have to maintain.

This thing, too, came as a surprise, or at least a surprise to the general public who are unaware of the workings of diplomacy. Those who know about such things were fully aware of what would happen if a whole lot of British sailors and diplomatists and journalists were exposed to the hospitalities of Washington. The British and Americans are both alike. You can't drive them or lead them or coerce them, but if you give them a cigar they'll do anything.

The inner history of the conference is only just beginning to be known. But it is whispered that immediately on his arrival Mr Balfour was given a cigar by President Harding. Mr Balfour at once offered to scrap five ships, and invited the entire American cabinet into the British Embassy, where Sir A. Geddes was rash enough to offer them champagne.

The American delegates immediately offered to scrap ten ships. Mr Balfour, who simply cannot be outdone in international courtesy, saw the ten and raised it to twenty. President Harding saw the twenty, raised it to thirty, and sent out for more poker chips

At the close of the play Lord Beatty, who is urbanity itself, offered to scrap Portsmouth Dockyard, and asked if anybody present would like Canada. President Harding replied with his customary tact that if England wanted the Philippines, he would think it what he would term a residuum of normalcy to give them away. There is no telling what might have happened had not Mr Briand interposed to say that any transfer of the Philippines must be regarded as a signal for a twenty per cent increase in the Boy Scouts of France. As a tactful conclusion to the matter President Harding raised Mr Balfour to the peerage.

As things are, disarmament coming along with the Irish settlement leaves English politics in a bad way. The general outlook is too peaceful altogether. One looks round almost in vain for any of those "strained relations" which used to be the very basis of English foreign policy. In only one direction do I see light for English politics, and that is over towards Czechoslovakia. It appears that Czechoslovakia owes the British Exchequer fifty million sterling. I cannot quote the exact figure, but it is either fifty million or fifty billion. In either case Czechoslovakia is unable to pay. The announcement has just been made by M. Sgitzch, the new treasurer, that the country is bankrupt or at least that he sees his way to make it so in a week.

It has been at once reported in City circles that there are "strained relations" between Great Britain and Czechoslovakia. Now what I advise is, that if the relations are strained, keep them so. England has lost nearly all the strained relations she ever had; let her cherish the few that she still has. I know that there are other opinions. The suggestion has been at once made for a "round table conference," at which the whole thing can be freely discussed without formal protocols and something like a "gentleman's agreement" reached. I say, don't do it. England is being ruined by these round table conferences. They are sitting round in Cairo and Calcutta and Capetown, filling all the best hotels and eating out the substance of the taxpayer.

I am told that Lloyd George has offered to go to Czechoslovakia. He should be stopped. It is said that Professor Keynes has proved that the best way to deal with the debt of Czechoslovakia is to send them whatever cash we have left, thereby turning the exchange upside down on them, and forcing them to buy all their Christmas presents in Manchester.

It is wiser not to do anything of the sort. England should send them a good old-fashioned ultimatum, mobilize all the naval officers at the Embankment hotels, raise the income tax another sixpence, and defy them.

If that were done it might prove a successful first step in bringing English politics back to the high plane of conversational interest from which they are threatening to fall.

Oxford

AS

I

SEE

IT

My private station being that of a university professor, I was naturally deeply interested in the system of education in England. I was therefore led to make a special visit to Oxford and to submit the place to a searching scrutiny. Arriving one afternoon at four o'clock, I stayed at the Mitre Hotel and did not leave until eleven o'clock next morning. The whole of this time, except for one hour spent in addressing the undergraduates, was devoted to a close and eager study of the great university. When I add to this that I had already visited Oxford in 1907 and spent a Sunday at All Souls with Colonel L. S. Amery, it will be seen at once that my views on Oxford are based upon observations extending over fourteen years.

At any rate I can at least claim that my acquaintance with the British university is just as good a basis for reflection and judgement as that of the numerous English critics who come to our side of the water. I have known a famous English writer to arrive at Harvard University in the morning, have lunch with President Lowell, and then write a whole chapter on the Excellence of Higher Education in America. I have known another one come to Harvard, have lunch with President Lowell, and do an entire book on the Decline of Serious Study in America. Or take the case of my own university. I remember Mr Rudyard Kipling coming to McGill and saying in his address to the undergraduates at 2.30 P.M., "You have here a great institution."

But how could he have gathered this information? As far as I know he spent the entire morning with Sir Andrew Macphail in his house beside the campus, smoking cigarettes. When I add that he distinctly refused to visit the Palaeontologic Museum, that he saw nothing of our new hydraulic apparatus, or of our classes in Domestic Science, his judgement that we had here a great institution seems a little bit superficial. I can only put beside it, to redeem it in some measure, the hasty and ill-formed judgement expressed by Lord Milner, "McGill is a noble university": and the rash and indiscreet expression of the Prince of Wales, when we give him an LL.D. degree, "McGill has a glorious future."

To my mind these unthinking judgements about our great college do harm, and I determined, therefore, that anything that I said about Oxford should be the result of the actual observation and real study based upon a bona fide residence in the Mitre Hotel.

On the strength of this basis of experience I am prepared to make the following positive and emphatic statements. Oxford is a noble university. It has a great past. It is at present the greatest university in the world: and it is quite possible that it has a great future. Oxford trains scholars of the real type better than any other place in the world. Its methods are antiquated. It despises science. Its lectures are rotten. It has professors who never teach and students who never learn. It has no order, no arrangement, no system. Its curriculum is unintelligible. It has no president. It has no state legislature to tell it how to teach, and yet—it gets there.

Whether we like it or not, Oxford gives something to its students, a life and a mode of thought, which in America as yet we can emulate but not equal.

If anybody doubts this let him go and take a room at the Mitre Hotel (ten and six for a wainscotted bedroom, period of Charles I) and study the place for himself.

These singular results achieved at Oxford are all the more surprising when one considers the distressing conditions under which the students work. The lack of an adequate building fund compels them to go on working in the same old buildings which they have had for centuries. The buildings at Brasenose College have not been renewed since the year 1525. In New College and Magdalen the students are still housed in old buildings erected in the sixteenth century. At Christ Church I was shown a kitchen which had been built at the expense of Cardinal Wolsey in 1527. Incredible though it may seem, they have no other place to cook in than this and are compelled to use it today. On the day when I saw this kitchen, four cooks were busy roasting an ox whole for the students' lunch: this at least is what I presumed they were doing from the size of the fireplace used, but it may not have been an ox; perhaps it was a cow. On a huge table, twelve feet by six and made of slabs of wood five inches thick, two other cooks were rolling out a game pie. I estimated it as measuring three feet across. In this rude way, unchanged since the time of Henry VIII, the unhappy Oxford students are fed. I could not help contrasting it with the cosy little boarding houses on Cottage Grove Avenue where I used to eat when I was a student at Chicago, or the charming little basement dining-rooms of the students' boarding houses in Toronto. But then, of course, Henry VIII never lived in Toronto.

The same lack of a building fund necessitates the Oxford students living in the identical old boarding houses they had in the sixteenth and seventeenth centuries. Technically they are called "quadrangles," "closes" and "rooms"; but I am so broken in to the usage of my student days that I can't help calling them boarding houses. In many of these the old stairway has been worn down by the feet of ten generations of students: the windows have little latticed panes: there are old names carved here and there upon the stone, and a thick growth of ivy covers the walls. The boarding house at St John's College dates from 1509, the one at Christ Church from the same period. A few hundred thousand pounds would suffice to replace these old buildings with neat steel and brick structures like the normal school at Schenectady, N. Y., or the Peel Street High School at Montreal. But nothing is done. A movement was indeed attempted last autumn towards removing the ivy from the walls, but the result was unsatisfactory and they are putting it back. Anyone could have told them beforehand that the mere removal of the ivy would not brighten Oxford up, unless at the same time one cleared the stones of the old inscriptions, put in steel fire escapes, and in fact brought the boarding houses up to date.

But Henry VIII being dead, nothing was done. Yet in spite of its dilapidated buildings and its lack of fire escapes, ventilation, sanitation, and up-to-date kitchen facilities, I persist in my assertion that I believe that Oxford, in its way, is the greatest university in the world. I am aware that this is an extreme statement and needs explanation. Oxford is much smaller in numbers, for example, than the State University of Minnesota, and is much poorer. It has, or had till yesterday, fewer students than the University of Toronto. To mention Oxford beside the 26,000 students of Columbia University sounds ridiculous. In point of money, the $39,000,000 endowment of the University of Chicago, and the $35,000,000 one of Columbia, and the $43,000,000 of Harvard seem to leave Oxford nowhere. Yet the peculiar thing is that it is not nowhere. By some queer process of its own it seems to get there every time. It was therefore of the very greatest interest to me, as a profound scholar, to try to investigate just how this peculiar excellence of Oxford arises.

It can hardly be due to anything in the curriculum or program of studies. Indeed, to anyone accustomed to the best models of a university curriculum as it flourishes in the United States and Canada, the program of studies is frankly quite laughable. There is less Applied Science in the place than would be found with us in a theological college. Hardly a single professor at Oxford would recognize a dynamo if he met it in broad daylight. The Oxford student learns nothing of chemistry, physics, heat, plumbing, electric wiring, gas fitting or the use of a blow torch. Any American college student can run a motor car, take a gasoline engine to pieces, fix a washer on a kitchen tap, mend a broken electric bell, and give an expert opinion on what has gone wrong with the furnace. It is these things indeed which stamp him as a college man, and occasion a very pardonable pride in the minds of his parents. But in all these things the Oxford student is the merest amateur.

This is bad enough. But after all one might say this is only the mechanical side of education. True: but one searches in vain in the Oxford curriculum for any adequate recognition of the higher and more cultured studies. Strange though it seems to us on this side of the Atlantic, there are no courses at Oxford in House-keeping, or in Salesmanship, or in Advertising, or on Comparative Religion, or on the influence of the Press. There are no lectures whatever on Human Behaviour, on Altruism, on Egotism, or on the Play of Wild Animals. Apparently, the Oxford student does not learn these things. This cuts him off from a great deal of the larger culture of our side of the Atlantic. "What are you studying this year?" I once asked a fourth-year student at one of our great colleges. "I am electing Salesmanship and Religion," he answered. Here was a young man whose training was destined inevitably to turn him into a moral businessman: either that or nothing. At Oxford, Salesmanship is not taught and Religion takes the feeble form of the New Testament. The more one looks at these things the more amazing it becomes that Oxford can produce any results at all.

The effect of the comparison is heightened by the peculiar position occupied at Oxford by the professors' lectures. In the colleges of Canada and the United States the lectures are supposed to be a really necessary and useful part of the students' training. Again and again I have heard the graduates of my own college assert that they had got as much, or nearly as much, out of the lectures at college as out of athletics or the Greek letter society or the Banjo and Mandolin Club. In short, with us the lectures form a real part of the college life. At Oxford it is not so. The lectures, I understand, are given and may even be taken. But they are quite worthless and are not supposed to have anything much to do with the development of the student's mind. "The lectures here," said a Canadian student to me, "are punk." I appealed to another student to know if this was so. "I don't know whether I'd call them exactly punk," he answered, "but they're certainly rotten." Other judgements were that the lectures were of no importance: that nobody took them: that they don't matter: that you can take them if you like: that they do you no harm.

It appears further that the professors themselves are not keen on their lectures. If the lectures are called for they give them; if not, the professor's feelings are not hurt. He merely waits and rests his brain until in some later year the students call for his lectures. There are men at Oxford who have rested their brains this way for over thirty years: the accumulated brain power thus dammed up is said to be colossal.

I understand that the key to this mystery is found in the operations of the person called the tutor. It is from him, or rather with him, that the students learn all that they know: one and all are agreed on that. Yet it is a little odd to know just how he does it. "We go over to his rooms," said one student, "and he just lights a pipe and talks to us." "We sit round with him," said another, "and he simply smokes and goes over our exercises with us." From this and other evidence I gather that what an Oxford tutor does is to get a little group of students together and smoke at them. Men who have been systematically smoked at for four years turn into ripe scholars. If anybody doubts this, let him go to Oxford and he can see the thing actually in operation. A well-smoked man speaks and writes English with a grace that can be acquired in no other way.

In what was said above, I seem to have been directing criticism against the Oxford professors as such: but I have no intention of doing so. For the Oxford professor and his whole manner of being I have nothing but a profound respect. There is indeed the greatest difference between the modern up-to-date American idea of a professor and the English type. But even with us in older days, in the bygone time when such people as Henry Wadsworth Longfellow were professors, one found the English idea; a professor was supposed to be a venerable kind of person, with snow-white whiskers reaching to his stomach. He was expected to moon about the campus oblivious of the world around him. If you nodded to him he failed to see you. Of money he knew nothing; of business, far less. He was, as his trustees were proud to say of him, "a child."

On the other hand he contained within him a reservoir of learning of such depth as to be practically bottomless. None of this learning was supposed to be of any material or commercial benefit to anybody. Its use was in saving the soul and enlarging the mind.

At the head of such a group of professors was one whose beard was even whiter and longer, whose absence of mind was even still greater, and whose knowledge of money, business, and practical affairs was below zero. Him they made the president.

All this is changed in America. A university professor is now a busy, hustling person, approximating as closely to a businessman as he can do it. It is on the businessman that he models himself. He has a little place that he calls his "office," with a typewriter machine and a stenographer. Here he sits and dictates letters, beginning after the best business models, "in re yours of the eighth ult., would say, etc., etc." He writes these letters to students, to his fellow professors, to the president, indeed to any people who will let him write to them. The number of letters that he writes each month is duly counted and set to his credit. If he writes enough he will get a reputation as an "executive," and big things may happen to him. He may even be asked to step out of the college and take a post as an "executive" in a soap company or an advertising firm. The man, in short, is a "hustler," an "advertiser" whose highest aim is to be a "live wire." If he is not, he will presently be dismissed, or, to use the business term, be "let go," by a board of trustees who are themselves hustlers and live wires. As to the professor's soul, he no longer needs to think of it as it has been handed over along with all the others to a Board of Censors.

The American professor deals with his students

according to his lights. It is his business to chase them along over a prescribed ground at a prescribed pace like a flock of sheep. They all go humping together over the hurdles with the professor chasing them with a set of "tests" and "recitations," "marks" and "attendances," the whole apparatus obviously copied from the time-clock of the businessman's factory. This process is what is called "showing results." The pace set is necessarily that of the slowest, and thus results in what I have heard Mr Edward Beatty describe as the "convoy system of education."

In my own opinion, reached after fifty-two years of profound reflection, this system contains in it-self the seeds of destruction. It puts a premium on dull-ness and a penalty on genius. It circumscribes that lat-itude of mind which is the real spirit of learning. If we persist in it we shall presently find that true learning will fly away from our universities and will take rest wherever some individual and inquiring mind can mark out its path for itself.

Now the principal reason why I am led to admire Oxford is that the place is little touched as yet by the measuring of "results," and by this passion for visible and provable "efficiency." The whole system at Oxford is such as to put a premium on genius and to let mediocrity and dullness go their way. On the dull stu-dent Oxford, after a proper lapse of time, confers a degree which means nothing more than that he lived and breathed at Oxford and kept out of jail. This for many students is as much as society can expect. But for the gifted student Oxford offers great opportunities.

There is no question of his hanging back till the last sheep has jumped over the fence. He need wait for no one. He may move forward as fast as he likes, following the bent of his genius. If he has in him any ability beyond that of the common herd, his tutor, interested in his studies, will smoke at him until he kindles him into a flame. For the tutor's soul is not harassed by herding dull students, with dismissal hanging by a thread over his head in the classroom. The American professor has no time to be interested in a clever student. He has time to be interested in his "deportment," his letter writing, his executive work, and his organizing ability and his hope of promotion to a soap factory. But with that his mind is exhausted. The student of genius merely means to him a student who gives no trouble, who passes all his "tests," and is present at all his "recitations." Such a student also, if he can be trained to be a hustler and an advertiser, will undoubtedly "make good." But beyond that the professor does not think of him. The everlasting principle of equality has inserted itself in a place where it has no right to be, and where inequality is the breath of life.

American or Canadian college trustees would be horrified at the notion of professors who apparently do no work, give few or no lectures and draw their pay merely for existing. Yet these are really the only kind of professors worth having—I mean, men who can be trusted with a vague general mission in life, with a salary guaranteed at least till their death, and a sphere of duties entrusted solely to their own consciences and the promptings of their own desires. Such men are rare, but a single one of them, when found, is worth ten "executives" and a dozen "organizers."

The excellence of Oxford, then, as I see it, lies in the peculiar vagueness of the organization of its work. It starts from the assumption that the professor is a really learned man whose sole interest lies in his own sphere: and that a student, or at least the only student with whom the university cares to reckon seriously, is a young man who desires to know. This is an ancient mediaeval attitude long since buried in more up-to-date places under successive strata of compulsory education, state teaching, the democratization of knowledge and the substitution of the shadow for the substance, and the casket for the gem. No doubt, in newer places the thing has got to be so. Higher education in America flourishes chiefly as a qualification for entrance into a money-making profession, and not as a thing in itself. But in Oxford one can still see the surviving outline of a nobler type of structure and a higher inspiration.

I do not mean to say, however, that my judgement of Oxford is one undiluted stream of praise. In one respect at least I think that Oxford has fallen away from the high ideals of the Middle Ages. I refer to the fact that it admits women students to its studies. In the Middle Ages women were regarded with a peculiar chivalry long since lost. It was taken for granted that their brains were too delicately poised to allow them to learn anything. It was presumed that their minds were so exquisitely hung that intellectual effort might disturb them. The present age has gone to the other extreme: and this is seen nowhere more than in the crowding of women into colleges originally designed for men. Oxford, I regret to find, has not stood out against this change.

To a profound scholar like myself, the presence of these young women, many of them most attractive, flittering up and down the streets of Oxford in their caps and gowns, is very distressing.

Who is to blame for this and how they first got in I do not know. But I understand that they first of all built a private college of their own close to Oxford, and then edged themselves in foot by foot. If this is so they only followed up the precedent of the recognized method in use in America. When an American college is established, the women go and build a college of their own overlooking the grounds. Then they put on becoming caps and gowns and stand and look over the fence at the college athletics. The male undergraduates, who were originally and by nature a hardy lot, were not easily disturbed. But inevitably some of the senior trustees fell in love with the first year girls and became convinced that coeducation was a noble cause. American statistics show that between 1880 and 1900 the number of trustees and senior professors who married girl undergraduates or who wanted to do so reached a percentage of—I forget the exact percentage; it was either a hundred or a little over.

I don't know just what happened at Oxford but presumably something of the sort took place. In any case the women are now all over the place. They attend the college lectures, they row in a boat, and they perambulate the High Street. They are even offering a serious competition against the men. Last year they carried off the ping-pong championship and took the chancellor's prize for needlework, while in music, cooking and millinery the men are said to be nowhere.

There is no doubt that unless Oxford puts the women out while there is yet time, they will overrun the whole university. What this means to the progress of learning few can tell and those who know are afraid to say.

Cambridge University, I am glad to see, still sets its face sternly against this innovation. I am reluctant to count any superiority in the University of Cambridge. Having twice visited Oxford, having made the place a subject of profound study for many hours at a time, having twice addressed its undergraduates, and having stayed at the Mitre Hotel, I consider myself an Oxford man. But I must admit that Cambridge has chosen the wiser part.

Last autumn, while I was in London on my voyage of discovery, a vote was taken at Cambridge to see if the women who have already a private college nearby should be admitted to the university. They were triumphantly shut out; and as a fit and proper sign of enthusiasm the undergraduates went over in a body and knocked down the gates of the women's college. I know that it is a terrible thing to say that anyone approved of this. All the London papers came out with headings that read—ARE OUR UNDERGRADUATES TURNING INTO BABOONS? and so on. The *Manchester Guardian* draped its pages in black and even the London *Morning Post* was afraid to take bold ground in the matter. But

I do know also that there was a great deal of secret chuckling and jubilation in the London clubs. Nothing was expressed openly. The men of England have been too terrorized by the women for that. But in safe corners of the club, out of earshot of the waiters and away from casual strangers, little groups of elderly men chuckled quietly together. "Knocked down their gates, eh?" said the wicked old men to one another, and then whispered guiltily behind an uplifted hand, "Serve 'em right." Nobody dared to say anything outside. If they had someone would have got up and asked a question in the House of Commons. When this is done all England falls flat upon its face.

But for my part when I heard of the Cambridge vote, I felt as Lord Chatham did when he said in Parliament, "Sir, I rejoice that America has resisted." For I have long harboured views of my own upon the higher education of women. In these days, however, it requires no little hardihood to utter a single word of criticism against it. It is like throwing half a brick through the glass roof of a conservatory. It is bound to make trouble. Let me hasten, therefore, to say that I believe most heartily in the higher education of women; in fact, the higher the better. The only question to my mind is: What is "higher education" and how do you get it? With which goes the secondary inquiry, What is a woman and is she just the same as a man? I know that it sounds a terrible thing to say in these days, but I don't believe she is.

Let me say also that when I speak of coeducation I speak of what I know. I was coeducated myself some thirty-five years ago, at the very beginning of the thing. I learned my Greek alongside of a bevy of beauty on the opposite benches that mashed up the irregular verbs for us very badly. Incidentally, those girls are all married long since, and all the Greek they know now you could put under a thimble. But of that presently.

I have had further experience as well. I spent three years in the graduate school of Chicago, where co-educational girls were as thick as autumn leaves—and some thicker. And as a college professor at McGill University in Montreal, I have taught mingled classes of men and women for twenty years.

On the basis of which experience I say with assurance that the thing is a mistake and has nothing to recommend it but its relative cheapness. Let me emphasize this last point and have done with it. Coeducation is of course a great economy. To teach ten men and ten women in a single class of twenty costs only half as much as to teach two classes. Where economy must rule, then, the thing has got to be. But where the discussion turns not on what is cheapest, but on what is best, then the case is entirely different.

The fundamental trouble is that men and women are different creatures, with different minds and different aptitudes and different paths in life. There is no need to raise here the question of which is superior and which is inferior (though I think, the Lord help me, I know the answer to that too). The point lies in the fact that they are different.

But the mad passion for equality has masked this obvious fact. When women began to demand, quite rightly, a share in higher education, they took for granted that they wanted the same curriculum as the men. They never stopped to ask whether their aptitudes were not in various directions higher and better than those of the men, and whether it might not be better for their sex to cultivate the things which were best suited to their minds. Let me be more explicit. In all that goes with physical and mathematical science, women, on the average, are far below the standard of men. There are, of course, exceptions. But they prove nothing. It is no use to quote to me the case of some brilliant girl who stood first in physics at Cornell. That's nothing. There is an elephant in the zoo that can count up to ten, yet I refuse to reckon myself his inferior.

Tabulated results spread over years, and the actual experience of those who teach show that in the whole domain of mathematics and physics women are outclassed. At McGill the girls of our first year have wept over their failures in elementary physics these twenty-five years. It is time that someone dried their tears and took away the subject.

But, in any case, examination tests are never the whole story. To those who know, a written examination is far from being a true criterion of capacity. It demands too much of mere memory, imitativeness, and the insidious willingness to absorb other people's ideas. Parrots and crows would do admirably in examinations. Indeed, the colleges are full of them.

But take, on the other hand, all that goes with the aesthetic side of education, with imaginative literature and the cult of beauty. Here women are, or at least ought to be, the superiors of men. Women were in primitive times the first story-tellers. They are still so at the cradle side. The original college woman was the witch, with her incantations and her prophecies and the glow of her bright imagination, and if brutal men of duller brains had not burned it out of her, she would be incanting still. To my thinking, we need more witches in the colleges and less physics.

I have seen such young witches myself—if I may keep the word: I like it—in colleges such as Wellesley in Massachusetts and Bryn Mawr in Pennsylvania, where there isn't a man allowed within the three-mile limit. To my mind, they do infinitely better thus by themselves. They are freer, less restrained. They discuss things openly in their classes; they lift up their voices, and they speak, whereas a girl in such a place as McGill, with men all about her, sits for four years as silent as a frog full of shot.

But there is a deeper trouble still. The careers of the men and women who go to college together are necessarily different, and the preparation is all aimed at the man's career. The men are going to be lawyers, doctors, engineers, businessmen, and politicians. And the women are not.

There is no use pretending about it. It may sound an awful thing to say, but the women are going to be married. That is, and always has been, their career; and, what is more, they know it; and even at college, while they are studying algebra and political economy, they have their eye on it sideways all the time. The plain fact is that, after a girl has spent four years of her time and a great deal of her parents' money in equipping herself for a career that she is never going to have, the wretched creature goes and gets married, and in a few years she has forgotten which is the hypotenuse of a right-angled triangle, and she doesn't care. She has much better things to think of.

At this point someone will shriek: "But surely, even for marriage, isn't it right that a girl should have a college education?" To which I hasten to answer: most assuredly. I freely admit that a girl who knows algebra, or once knew it, is a far more charming companion and a nobler wife and mother than a girl who doesn't know x from y. But the point is this: Does the higher education that fits a man to be a lawyer also fit a person to be a wife and mother? Or, in other words, is a lawyer a wife and mother? I say he is not. Granted that a girl is to spend four years in time and four thousand dollars in money in going to college, why train her for a career that she is never going to adopt? Why not give her an education that will have a meaning and a harmony with the real life that she is to follow?

For example, suppose that during her four years every girl lucky enough to get a higher education spent at least six months of it in the training and discipline of a hospital as a nurse. There is more education and character making in that than in a whole bucketful of algebra.

But no, the woman insists on snatching her share of an education designed by Erasmus or William of Wykeham or William of Occam for the creation of scholars and lawyers; and when later on in her home there is a sudden sickness or accident, and the life or death of those nearest to her hangs upon the skill and knowledge and a trained fortitude in emergency, she must needs send in all haste for a hired woman to fill the place that she herself has never learned to occupy.

But I am not here trying to elaborate a whole curriculum. I am only trying to indicate that higher education for the man is one thing, for the woman another. Nor do I deny the fact that women have got to earn their living. Their higher education must enable them to do that. They cannot all marry on their graduation day. But that is no great matter. No scheme of education that anyone is likely to devise will fail in this respect.

The positions that they hold as teachers or civil servants they would fill better if their education were fitted to their wants.

Some few, a small minority, really and truly "have a career"—husbandless and childless—in which the sacrifice is great and the honour to them, perhaps, all the higher. And others no doubt dream of a career in which a husband and a group of blossoming children are carried as an appendage to a busy life at the bar or on the platform. But all such are the mere minority, so small as to make no difference to the general argument.

But there—I have written quite enough to make plenty of trouble except perhaps at Cambridge University. So I turn with relief to my general study of Oxford. Viewing the situation as a whole, I am led then to the conclusion that there must be something in the life of Oxford itself that makes for higher learning.

Smoked at by his tutor, fed in Henry VIII's kitchen, and sleeping in a tangle of ivy, the student evidently gets something not easily obtained in America. And the more I reflect on the matter the more I am convinced that it is the sleeping in the ivy that does it. How different it is from student life as I remember it!

When I was a student at the University of Toronto thirty years ago, I lived—from start to finish—in seventeen different boarding houses. As far as I am aware these houses have not, or not yet, been marked with tablets. But they are still to be found in the vicinity of McCaul and Darcy and St Patrick Streets. Anyone who doubts the truth of what I have to say may go and look at them.

I was not alone in the nomadic life that I led. There were hundreds of us drifting about in this fashion from one melancholy habitation to another. We lived as a rule two or three in a house, sometimes alone. We dined in the basement. We always had beef, done up in some way after it was dead, and there were always soda biscuits on the table. They used to have a brand of soda biscuits in those days in the Toronto boarding houses that I have not seen since. They were better than dog biscuits but with not so much snap. My contemporaries will all remember them. A great many of the leading barristers and professional men of Toronto were fed on them.

In the life we led we had practically no opportunities for association on a large scale, no common rooms, no reading rooms, nothing. We never saw the magazines—personally I didn't even know the names of them. The only interchange of ideas we ever got was by going over to the Caer Howell Hotel on University Avenue and interchanging them there.

I mention these melancholy details not for their own sake but merely to emphasize the point that when I speak of students' dormitories, and the larger life which they offer, I speak of what I know.

If we had had at Toronto, when I was a student, the kind of dormitories and dormitory life that they have at Oxford, I don't think I would ever have graduated. I'd have been there still. The trouble is that the universities on our continent are only just waking up to the idea of what a university should mean. They were, very largely, instituted and organized with the idea that a university was a place where young men were sent to absorb the contents of books and to listen to lectures in the class rooms. The student was pictured as a pallid creature, burning what was called the "midnight oil," his wan face bent over his desk. If you wanted to do something for him you gave him a book : if you wanted to do something really large on his behalf you gave him a whole basketful of them. If you wanted to go still further and be a benefactor to the college at large, you endowed a competitive scholarship and set two or more pallid students working themselves to death to get it.

The real thing for the student is the life and environment that surrounds him. All that he really learns he learns, in a sense, by the active operation of his own intellect and not as the passive recipient of lectures. And for this active operation what he really needs most is the continued and intimate contact with his fellows.

Students must live together and eat together, talk and smoke together. Experience shows that that is how their minds really grow. And they must live together in a rational and comfortable way. They must eat in a big dining room or hall, with oak beams across the ceiling, and the stained glass in the windows, and with a shield or tablet here or there upon the wall, to remind them between times of the men who went before them and left a name worthy of the memory of the college. If a student is to get from his college what it ought to give him, a college dormitory, with the life in common that it brings, is his absolute right. A university that fails to give it to him is cheating him.

If I were founding a university—and I say it with all the seriousness of which I am capable—I would found first a smoking room; then when I had a little more money in hand I would found a dormitory; then after that, or more probably with it, a decent reading room and a library. After that, if I still had money over that I couldn't use, I would hire a professor and get some textbooks.

This chapter has sounded in the most part like a continuous eulogy of Oxford with but little in favour of our American colleges. I turn therefore with pleasure to the more congenial task of showing what is wrong with Oxford and with the English university system generally, and the aspect in which our American universities far excel the British.

The point is that Henry VIII is dead. The English are so proud of what Henry VIII and the benefactors of earlier centuries did for the universities that they forget the present. There is little or nothing in England to compare with the magnificent generosity of individuals, provinces and states, which is building up the colleges of the United States and Canada. There used to be. But by some strange confusion of thought the English people admire the noble gifts of Cardinal Wolsey and Henry VIII and Queen Margaret, and do not realize that the Carnegies and Rockefellers and the William Macdonalds are the Cardinal Wolseys of today. The University of Chicago was founded upon oil. McGill University rests largely on a basis of tobacco. In America the world of commerce and business levies on itself a noble tribute in favour of the higher learning. In England, with a few conspicuous exceptions, such as that at Bristol, there is little of the sort. The feudal families are content with what their remote ancestors have done: they do not try to emulate it in any great degree.

In the long run this must count. Of all the various reforms that are talked of at Oxford, and of all the imitations of American methods that are suggested, the only one worth while, to my thinking, is to capture a few millionaires, give them honorary degrees at a million pounds sterling apiece, and tell them to imagine that they are Henry VIII. I give Oxford warning that if this is not done the place will not last another two centuries.

THE BRITISH

THE AMERICAN

PRESS

The only paper from which a man can really get the news of the world in a shape that he can understand is the newspaper of his own "home town." For me, unless I can have the Montreal *Gazette* at my breakfast, and the Montreal *Star* at my dinner, I don't really know what is happening. In the same way I have seen a man from the south of Scotland settle down to read the *Dumfries Chronicle* with a deep sigh of satisfaction: and a man from Burlington, Vermont, pick up the Burlington *Eagle* and study the foreign news in it as the only way of getting at what was really happening in France and Germany.

The reason is, I suppose, that there are different ways of serving up the news and we each get used to our own. Some people like the news fed to them gently: others like it thrown at them in a bombshell: some prefer it to be made as little of as possible; they want it minimized: others want the maximum.

This is where the greatest difference lies between the British newspapers and those of the United States and Canada. With us in America the great thing is to get the news and shout it at the reader; in England they get the news and then break it to him as gently as possible. Hence the big headings, the bold type, and the double columns of the American paper, and the small headings and the general air of quiet and respectability of the English Press.

It is quite beside the question to ask which is

the better. Neither is. They are different things: that's all. The English newspaper is designed to be read quietly, propped up against the sugar bowl of a man eating a slow breakfast in a quiet corner of a club, or by a retired banker seated in a leather chair nearly asleep, or by a country vicar sitting in a wicker chair under a pergola. The American paper is for reading by a man hanging on the straps of a clattering subway express, by a man eating at a lunch counter, by a man standing on one leg, by a man getting a two-minute shave, or by a man about to have his teeth drawn by a dentist.

In other words, there is a difference of atmosphere. It is not merely in the type of the lettering, it is a difference in the way the news is treated and the kind of words that are used. In America we love such words as "gun men" and "joy ride" and "death cell"; in England they prefer "person of doubtful character" and "motor travelling at excessive speed" and "corridor No. 6." If a milk wagon collides in the street with a coal cart, we write that a "life wagon" has struck a "death cart." We call a murderer a "thug" or a "gun man" or a "yegg man." In England they simply call him "the accused who is a grocer's assistant in Houndsditch." That designation would knock any decent murder story to pieces.

Hence comes the great difference between the American "lead" or opening sentence of the article, and the English method of commencement. In the American paper the idea is that the reader is so busy that he must first be offered the news in one gulp. After that if he likes it he can go on and eat some more of it. So the opening sentence must give the whole thing. Thus, suppose that a leading member of the United States Congress has committed suicide. This is the way in which the American reporter deals with it.

"Seated in his room at the Grand Hotel with his carpet slippers on his feet and his body wrapped in a blue dressing gown with pink insertions, after writing a letter of farewell to his wife and emptying a bottle of Scotch whisky in which he exonerated her from all culpability in his death, Congressman Ahasuerus P. Tigg was found by night watchman Henry T. Smith, while making his rounds as usual with four bullets in his stomach."

Now let us suppose that a leading member of the House of Commons in England had done the same thing. Here is the way it would be written up in a first-class London newspaper. The heading would be HOME AND GENERAL INTELLIGENCE. That is inserted so as to keep the reader soothed and quiet and is no doubt thought better than the American heading BUGHOUSE CONGRESSMAN BLOWS OUT BRAINS IN HOTEL. After the heading HOME AND GENERAL INTELLIGENCE the English paper runs the subheading INCIDENT AT THE GRAND HOTEL. The reader still doesn't know what happened; he isn't meant to. Then the article begins like this:

"The Grand Hotel, which is situated at the corner of Millbank and Victoria Streets, was the scene last night of a distressing incident."

"What is it?" thinks the reader.

"The hotel itself, which is an old Georgian structure dating probably from about 1750, is a quiet establishment, its clientele mainly drawn from businessmen in the cattle-droving and distillery business from South Wales."

"What happened?" thinks the reader.

"Its cuisine has long been famous for the excellence of its boiled shrimps."

"What happened?"

"While the hotel itself is also known as the meeting place of the Surbiton Harmonic Society and other associations."

"What happened?"

"Among the more prominent of the guests of the hotel has been numbered during the present Parliamentary session Mr Llewylln Ap Jones, M.P. for South Llanfydd. Mr Jones apparently came to his room last night at about ten P.M., and put on his carpet slippers and his blue dressing gown. He then seems to have gone to the cupboard and taken from it a whisky bottle which however proved empty. The unhappy gentleman then apparently went to bed . . ."

At that point the American reader probably stops reading, thinking that he has heard it all. The unhappy man found that the bottle was empty and went to bed: very natural: and the affair very properly called a "distressing incident": quite right. But the trained English reader would know that there was more to come and that the air of quiet was only assumed, and he would read on and on until at last the tragic interest heightened, the four shots were fired, with a good long pause after each for discussion of the path of the bullet through Mr Ap Jones.

I am not saying that either the American way or the British way is the better. They are just two different ways, that's all. But the result is that anybody from the United States or Canada reading the English papers gets the impression that nothing is happening: and an English reader of our newspapers with us gets the idea that the whole place is in a tumult.

When I was in London I used always, in glancing at the morning papers, to get a first impression that the whole world was almost asleep. There was, for example, a heading called INDIAN INTELLIGENCE that showed, on close examination, that two thousand Parsees had died of the blue plague, that a powder boat had blown up at Bombay, that someone had thrown a couple of bombs at one of the provincial governors, and that four thousand agitators had been sentenced to twenty years hard labour each. But the whole thing was just called "Indian Intelligence." Similarly, there was a little item called "Our Chinese Correspondent." That one explained ten lines down, in very small type, that a hundred thousand Chinese had been drowned in a flood. And there was another little item labelled "Foreign Gossip," under which was mentioned that the Pope was dead, and that the President of Paraguay had been assassinated.

In short, I got the impression that I was living in an easy drowsy world, as no doubt the editor meant me to. It was only when the Montreal *Star* arrived by post that I felt that the world was still revolving pretty rapidly on its axis and that there was still something doing.

As with the world news so it is with the minor events of ordinary life—birth, death, marriage, accidents, crime. Let me give an illustration. Suppose that in a suburb of London a housemaid has endeavoured to poison her employer's family by putting a drug in the coffee. Now on our side of the water we should write that little incident up in a way to give it life, and put headings over it that would capture the reader's attention in a minute. We should begin it thus:

Pretty Parlour Maid Deals Death-drink to Clubman's Family

The English reader would ask at once, how do we know that the parlour maid is pretty? We don't. But our artistic sense tells us that she ought to be. Pretty parlour maids are the only ones we take any interest in: if an ugly parlour maid poisoned her employer's family we should hang her. Then again, the English reader would say, how do we know that the man is a clubman? Have we ascertained this fact definitely, and if so, of what club or clubs is he a member? Well, we don't know, except in so far as the thing is self-evident. Any man who has romance enough in his life to be poisoned by a pretty housemaid *ought* to be in a club. That's the place for him. In fact, with us the word clubman doesn't necessarily mean a man who belongs to a club; it is defined as a man who is arrested in a gambling den, or fined for speeding a motor or who shoots another person in a hotel corridor. Therefore this man must be a clubman. Having settled the heading, we go on with the text:

"Brooding over love troubles which she has hitherto refused to divulge under the most grilling fusillade of rapid-fire questions shot at her by the best brains of the New York police force, Miss Mary De Forrest, a handsome brunette thirty-six inches around the hips, employed as a parlour maid in the residence of Mr Spudd Bung, a well-known clubman forty-two inches around the chest, was arrested yesterday by the flying squad of the emergency police after having, so it is alleged, put four ounces of alleged picrate of potash into the alleged coffee of her employer's family's alleged breakfast at their residence on Hudson Heights in the most fashionable quarter of the metropolis. Dr Slink, the leading fashionable practitioner of the neighbourhood who was immediately summoned, said that but for his own extraordinary dexterity and promptness the death of the whole family, if not of the entire entourage, was a certainty. The magistrate in committing Miss De Forrest for trial took occasion to enlarge upon her youth and attractive appearance: he castigated the moving pictures severely and said that he held them together with the public school system and the present method of doing the hair, directly responsible for the crimes of the kind alleged."

Now when you read this over you begin to feel that something *big* has happened. Here is a man like Dr Slink, all quivering with promptness and dexterity. Here is an inserted picture, a photograph, a brick house in a row marked with a cross (×) and labelled "The Bung Residence as it appeared immediately after the alleged outrage." It isn't really. It is just a photograph that we use for this sort of thing and have grown to like. It is called sometimes "Residence of Senator Borah" or "Scene of the Recent Spiritualistic Manifestations" or anything of the sort. As long as it is marked with a cross (×) the reader will look at it with interest.

In other words we make something out of an occurrence like this. It doesn't matter if it all fades out afterwards when it appears that Mary De Forrest merely put ground allspice into the coffee in mistake for powdered sugar and that the family didn't drink it anyway. The reader has already turned to other mysteries.

But contrast the pitifully tame way in which the same event is written up in England. Here it is:

Suburban Item

Yesterday at the police court of Surbiton-on-Thames Mary Forrester, a servant in the employ of Mr. S. Bung, was taken into custody on a charge of having put a noxious preparation, possibly poison, into the coffee of her employer's family. The young woman was remanded for a week.

Look at that. Mary Forrester a servant? How wide was she round the chest? It doesn't say. Mr S. Bung? Of what club was he a member? None, apparently. Then who cares if he is poisoned? And "the young woman"! What a way to speak of a decent girl who never did any other harm than to poison a clubman. And the English magistrate! What a tame part he must have played : his name indeed doesn't occur at all : apparently he didn't enlarge on the girl's good looks, or "comment on her attractive appearance," or anything. I don't suppose that he even asked Mary Forrester out to lunch with him.

Notice also that, according to the English way of writing the thing up, as soon as the girl was remanded for a week the incident is closed. The English reporter doesn't apparently know enough to follow Miss De Forrest to her home (called "the De Forrest Residence" and marked with a cross, ×). The American reporter would make certain to supplement what went above with further information of this fashion. "Miss De Forrest when seen later at her own home by a representative of *The Eagle* said that she regretted very much having been put to the necessity of poisoning Mr Bung. She had in the personal sense nothing against Mr Bung and apart from poisoning him she had every respect for Mr Bung. Miss De Forrest, who talks admirably on a variety of topics, expressed herself as warmly in favour of the League of Nations and as a devotee of the short ballot and proportional representation."

Any American reader who studies the English Press comes upon these wasted opportunities every day. There are indeed certain journals of a newer type which are doing their best to imitate us. But they don't really get it yet. They use type up to about one inch and after that they get afraid.

I hope that in describing the spirit of the English Press I do not seem to be writing with any personal bitterness. I admit that there might be a certain reason for such a bias. During my stay in England I was most anxious to appear as a contributor to some of the leading papers. This is, with the English, a thing that always adds prestige. To be able to call oneself a "contributor" to *The Times* or to *Punch* or the *Morning Post* or the *Spectator* is a high honour. I have met these "contributors" all over the British Empire. Some, I admit, look strange. An ancient wreck in the back bar of an Ontario tavern (ancient régime) has told me that he was a contributor to *The Times* : the janitor of the building where I lived admits that he is a contributor to *Punch* : a man arrested in Bristol for vagrancy while I was in England pleaded that he was a contributor to the *Spectator*. In fact, it is an honour that everybody seems to be able to get but me.

I had often tried before I went to England to contribute to the great English newspapers. I had never succeeded. But I hoped that while in England itself the very propinquity of the atmosphere, I mean the very contiguity of the surroundings, would render the attempt easier. I tried and I failed. My failure was all the more ignominious in that I had very direct personal encouragement. "By all means," said the editor of the London *Times*, "do something for us while you are here. Best of all, do something in a political way; that's rather our special line." I had already received almost an identical encouragement from the London *Morning Post*, and in a more qualified way from the *Manchester Guardian*. In short, success seemed easy.

I decided therefore to take some simple political event of the peculiar kind that always makes a stir in English politics and write it up for these English papers. To simplify matters I thought it better to use one and the same incident and write it up in three different ways and get paid for it three times. All of those who write for the Press will understand the motive at once. I waited therefore and watched the papers to see if anything interesting might happen to the Ahkoond of Swat or the Sandjak of Novi Bazar or any other native potentate. Within a couple of days I got what I wanted in the following item, which I need hardly say is taken word for word from the Press dispatches:

Perim, via Bombay. News comes by messenger that the Shriek of Kowfat who has been living under the convention of 1898 has violated the *modus operandi.* He is said to have torn off his suspenders, dipped himself in oil and proclaimed a *Jehad.* The situation is critical.

Everybody who knows England knows that this is just the kind of news that the English love. On our side of the Atlantic we should be bothered by the fact that we did not know where Kowfat is, nor what was the convention of 1898. They are not. They just take it for granted that Kowfat is one of the many thousand places they "own," somewhere in the outer darkness. They have so many Kowfats that they cannot keep track of them.

I knew therefore that everybody would be interested in any discussion of what was at once called "the Kowfat Crisis" and I wrote it up. I resisted the temptation to begin after the American fashion, "Shriek sheds suspenders," and suited the writing, as I thought, to the market I was writing for. I wrote up the incident for the *Morning Post* after the following fashion:

The news from Kowfat affords one more instance of a painful back-down on the part of the Government. Our policy of spineless supineness is now reaping its inevitable reward. To us there is only one thing to be done. If the Shriek has torn off his suspenders he must be made to put them on again. We have always held that where the imperial prestige of this country is concerned there is no room for hesitation. In the present instance our prestige is at stake: the matter involves our reputation in the eyes of the surrounding natives, the Bantu Hottentots, the Negritos, the Dwarf Men of East Abyssinia, and the Dog Men of Darfur. What will they think of us? If we fail in this crisis their notion of us will fall fifty per cent. In our opinion this country cannot stand a fifty per cent drop in the estimation of the Dog Men. The time is one that demands action. An ultimatum should be sent at once to the Shriek of Kowfat. If he has one already we should send him another. He should be made at once to put on his suspenders. The oil must be scraped off him, and he must be told plainly that if a pup like him tries to start a Jehad he will have to deal with the British Navy. We call the Shriek a pup in no sense of belittling him as our imperial ally but because we consider that the present is no time for half words and we do not regard pup as half a word. Events such as the present, rocking the

Empire to its base, make one long for the spacious days of a Salisbury or a Queen Elizabeth, or an Alfred the Great or a Julius Caesar. We doubt whether the present Cabinet is in this class.

Not to lose any time in the coming and going of the mail, always a serious thought for the contributor to the Press waiting for a cheque. I sent another editorial on the same topic to the *Manchester Guardian*. It ran as follows :

The action of the Shriek of Kowfat in proclaiming a Jehad against us is one that amply justifies all that we have said editorially since Jeremy Bentham died. We have always held that the only way to deal with a Mohammedan potentate like the Shriek is to treat him like a Christian. The Khalifate of Kowfat at present buys its whole supply of cotton piece goods in our market and pays cash. The Shriek, who is a man of enlightenment, has consistently upheld the principles of Free Trade. Not only are our exports of cotton piece goods, Bibles, rum, and beads constantly increasing, but they are more than offset by our importation from Kowfat of ivory, rubber, gold, and oil. In short, we have never seen the principles of Free Trade better illustrated. The Shriek, it is now reported, refuses to wear the braces presented to him by our envoy at the time of his coronation five years ago. He is said to have thrown them into the mud. But we have no reason to suppose that this is meant as a blow at our prestige. It may be that after five years of use the little pulleys of the braces no longer work properly. We have ourselves in our personal life known instances of this, and can speak of the sense of irritation occasioned. Even we have thrown on the floor ours. And in any case, as we have often reminded our readers, what is prestige? If any one wants to hit us, let him hit us right there. We regard a blow at our trade as far more deadly than a blow at our prestige.

The situation as we see it demands immediate reparation on our part. The principal grievance of the Shriek arises from the existence of our fort and garrison on the Kowfat river. Our proper policy is to knock down the fort, and either remove the garrison or give it to the Shriek. We are convinced that as soon as the Shriek realizes that we are prepared to treat him in the proper Christian spirit, he will at once respond with true Mohammedan generosity.

We have further to remember that in what we do we are being observed by the neighbouring tribes, the Negritos, the Dwarf Men, and the Dog Men of Darfur. These are not only shrewd observers but substantial customers. The Dwarf Men at present buy all their cotton on the Manchester market and the Dog Men depend on us for their soap.

The present crisis is one in which the nation needs statesmanship and a broad outlook upon the world. In the existing situation we need not the duplicity of a Machiavelli, but the commanding prescience of a Gladstone or an Alfred the Great, or a

Julius Caesar. Luckily we have exactly this type of man at the head of affairs.

After completing the above I set to work without delay on a similar exercise for the London *Times*. The special excellence of *The Times*, as everybody knows, is its fulness of information. For generations past *The Times* has commanded a peculiar minuteness of knowledge about all parts of the Empire. It is the proud boast of this great journal that to whatever faraway, outlandish part of the Empire you may go, you will always find a correspondent of *The Times* looking for something to do. It is said that the present proprietor has laid it down as his maxim, "I don't want men who think; I want men who know." The arrangements for thinking are made separately.

Incidentally I may say that I had personal opportunities while I was in England of realizing that the reputation of the *Times* staff for the possession of information is well founded. Dining one night with some members of the staff, I happened to mention Saskatchewan. One of the editors at the other end of the table looked up at the mention of the name. "Saskatchewan," he said, "ah, yes; that's not far from Alberta, is it?" and then turned quietly to his food again. When I remind the reader that Saskatchewan is only half an inch from Alberta he may judge of the nicety of the knowledge involved. Having all this in mind, I recast the editorial and sent it to the London *Times* as follows:

The news that the Sultan of Kowfat has thrown away his suspenders renders it of interest to indicate the exact spot where he has thrown them. (See map.) Kowfat, lying as the reader knows, on the Kowfat River, occupies the hinterland between the back end of southwest Somaliland and the east, that is to say, the west, bank of Lake P'schu. It thus forms an enclave between the Dog Men of Darfur and the Negritos of T'chk. The inhabitants of Kowfat are a coloured race three quarters Negroid and more than three quarters tabloid.

As a solution of the present difficulty, the first thing required in our opinion is to send out a boundary commission to delineate more exactly still just where Kowfat is. After that an ethnographical survey might be completed.

It was a matter not only of concern but of surprise to me that not one of the three contributions recited above was accepted by the English Press. The *Morning Post* complained that my editorial was not firm enough in tone, the *Guardian* that it was not humane enough, the *Times* that I had left out the latitude and longitude always expected by their readers.

I thought it not worth while to bother to revise the articles as I had meantime conceived the idea that the same material might be used in the most delightfully amusing way as the basis of a poem for *Punch*. Everybody knows the kind of verses that are contributed to *Punch* by Sir Owen Seaman and Mr Charles Graves and men of that sort. And everybody has been struck, as I have, by the extraordinary easiness of the performance. All that one needs is to get some odd little incident, such as the revolt of the Sultan of Ķǫwfat, make up an amusing title, and then string the verses together in such a way as to make rhymes with all the odd words that come into the narrative. In fact, the thing is ease itself.

I therefore saw a glorious chance with the Sultan of Kowfat. Indeed, I fairly chuckled to myself when I thought what amusing rhymes could be made with "Negritos," "modus operandi" and " Dog Men of Darfur." I can scarcely imagine anything more excruciatingly funny than the rhymes which can be made with them. And as for the title, bringing in the word Kowfat or some play upon it, the thing is perfectly obvious. The idea amused me so much that I set to work at the poem at once. I am sorry to say that I failed to complete it. Not that I couldn't have done so, given time; I am quite certain that if I had had about two years I could have done it. The main structure of the poem, however, is here and I give it for what it is worth. Even as it is it strikes me as extraordinarily good. Here it is:

TITLE

.... Kowfat

VERSE ONE

....
.... modus operandi;
....
.... Negritos:
.... P'schu

....

....Khalifate;

.................................Dog Men of Darfur:

.... T'chk.

Excellent little thing, isn't it? All it needs is the rhymes. As far as it goes it has just exactly the ease and the sweep required. And if someone will tell me how Owen Seaman and those people get the rest of the ease and the sweep I'll be glad to put it in.

One further experiment of the same sort I made with the English Press in another direction and met again with failure. If there is one paper in the world for which I have respect and—if I may say it—an affection, it is the London *Spectator*. I suppose that I am only one of thousands and thousands of people who feel that way. Why under the circumstances the *Spectator* failed to publish my letter I cannot say. I wanted no money for it: I only wanted the honour of seeing it inserted beside the letter written from the Rectory, Hops, Hants, or the Pottery, Potts, Shrops—I mean from one of those places where the readers of the *Spectator* live. I thought too that my letter had just the right touch. However, they wouldn't take it: something wrong with it somewhere, I suppose. This is it:

To the Editor,
The *Spectator*,
London, England.
Dear Sir,

Your correspondence of last week contained such interesting information in regard to the appearance of the first cowslip in Kensington Common that I trust that I may, without fatiguing your readers to the point of saturation, narrate a somewhat similar and I think, sir, an equally interesting experience of my own. While passing through Lambeth Gardens yesterday towards the hour of dusk I observed a crow with one leg sitting beside the duck pond and apparently lost in thought. There was no doubt that the bird was of the species *pulex hibiscus*, an order which is becoming singularly rare in the vicinity of the metropolis. Indeed, so far as I am aware, the species has not been seen in London since 1680. I may say that on recognizing the bird I drew as near as I could, keeping myself behind the shrubbery, but the *pulex hibiscus* which apparently caught a brief glimpse of my face uttered a cry of distress and flew away.

I am, sir,
Believe me,
yours, sir,
O. Y. Botherwithit.
(Ret'd Major Burmese Army)

Distressed by these repeated failures, I sank back to a lower level of English literary work, the puzzle department. For some reason or other the English delight in puzzles. It is, I think, a part of the peculiar schoolboy pedantry which is the reverse side of their literary genius. I speak with a certain bitterness because in puzzle work I met with no success whatever. My solutions were never acknowledged, never paid for, in fact they were ignored. But I append two or three of them here, with apologies to the editors of the *Strand* and other papers who should have had the honour of publishing them first.

PUZZLE I

Can you fold a square piece of paper in such a way that with a single fold it forms a pentagon?

My Solution: Yes, if I knew what a pentagon was.

PUZZLE II

A and B agree to hold a walking match across an open meadow, each seeking the shortest line. A, walking from corner to corner, may be said to diangulate the hypotenuse of the meadow. B, allowing for a slight rise in the ground, walks on an obese tabloid. Which wins?

My Solution: Frankly, I don't know.

PUZZLE III

(With apologies to the *Strand*)

A rope is passed over a pulley. It has a weight at one end and a monkey at the other. There is the same length of rope on either side and equilibrium is maintained. The rope weighs four ounces per foot. The age of the monkey and the age of the monkey's mother together total four years. The weight of the monkey is as many pounds as the monkey's mother is years old. The monkey's mother was twice as old as the monkey was when the monkey's mother was half as old as the monkey will be when the monkey is three times as old as the monkey's mother was when the monkey's mother was three times as old as the monkey. The weight of the rope with the weight at the end was half as much again as the difference in weight between the weight of the weight and the weight of the monkey. Now, what was the length of the rope?

My Solution: I should think it would have to be a rope of a fairly good length.

In only one department of English journalism have I met with a decided measure of success—I refer to the juvenile competition department. This is a sort of thing to which the English are especially addicted. As a really educated nation for whom good literature begins in the home they encourage in every way literary competitions among the young readers of their journals. At least half a dozen of the well-known London periodicals carry on this work. The prizes run all the way from one shilling to half a guinea and the competitions are generally open to all children from three to six years of age. It was here that I saw my open opportunity and seized it. I swept in prize after prize. As "Little Agatha" I got four shillings for the best description of Autumn in two lines, and one shilling for guessing correctly the missing letters in BR–STOL, SH–FFIELD, and H–LL. A lot of the competitors fell down on H–LL. I got six shillings for giving the dates of the Norman Conquest—1492 A.D.—and the Crimean War of 1870. In short, the thing was easy. I might say that to enter these competitions one has to have a certificate of age from a member of the clergy. But I know a lot of them.

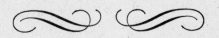

BUSINESS IN ENGLAND

WANTED:

MORE
PROFITEERS

It is hardly necessary to say that so shrewd an observer as I am could not fail to be struck by the situation of business in England. Passing through the factory towns and noticing that no smoke came from the tall chimneys and that the doors of the factories were shut, I was led to the conclusion that they were closed.

Observing that the streets of the industrial centres were everywhere filled with idle men, I gathered that they were unemployed: and when I learned that the moving picture houses were full to the doors every day and that the concert halls, beer gardens, grand opera, and religious concerts were crowded to suffocation, I inferred that the country was suffering from an unparalleled depression. This diagnosis turned out to be absolutely correct. It has been freely estimated that at the time I refer to almost two million men were out of work.

But it does not require government statistics to prove that in England at the present day everybody seems poor, just as in the United States everybody, to the eye of the visitor, seems to be rich. In England nobody seems to be able to afford anything: in the United States everybody seems to be able to afford everything. In England nobody smokes cigars: in America everybody does. On the English railways the first-class carriages are empty: in the United States the "reserved drawing-rooms" are full. Poverty no doubt is only a relative matter: but a man whose income used to be

£10,000 a year and is now £5,000, is living in "reduced circumstances"; he feels himself just as poor as the man whose income has been cut from five thousand pounds to three, or from five hundred pounds to two. They are all in the same boat. What with the lowering of dividends and the raising of the income tax, the closing of factories, feeding the unemployed and trying to employ the unfed, things are in a bad way.

The underlying cause is plain enough. The economic distress that the world suffers now is the inevitable consequence of the war. Everybody knows that. But where the people differ is in regard to what is going to happen next, and what we must do about it. Here opinion takes a variety of forms. Some people blame it on the German mark: by permitting their mark to fall, the Germans, it is claimed, are taking away all the business from England; the fall of the mark, by allowing the Germans to work harder and eat less than the English, is threatening to drive the English out of house and home: if the mark goes on falling still further the Germans will thereby outdo us also in music, literature and in religion. What has got to be done, therefore, is to force the Germans to lift the mark up again, and make them pay up their indemnity.

Another more popular school of thought holds to an entirely contrary opinion. The whole trouble, they say, comes from the sad collapse of Germany. These unhappy people, having been too busy for four years in destroying valuable property in France and Belgium to pay attention to their home affairs, now find themselves collapsed: it is our first duty to pick them up again. The

English should therefore take all the money they can find and give it to the Germans. By this means German trade and industry will revive to such an extent that the port of Hamburg will be its old bright self again and German waiters will reappear in the London hotels. After that everything will be all right.

Speaking with all the modesty of an outsider and a transient visitor, I give it as my opinion that the trouble is elsewhere. The danger of industrial collapse in England does not spring from what is happening in Germany but from what is happening in England itself. England, like most of the other countries in the world, is suffering from the over-extension of government and the decline of individual self-help. For six generations industry in England and America has flourished on individual effort called out by the prospect of individual gain. Every man acquired from his boyhood the idea that he must look after himself. Morally, physically and financially that was the recognized way of getting on. The desire to make a fortune was regarded as a laudable ambition, a proper stimulus to effort. The ugly word "profiteer" had not yet been coined. There was no income tax to turn a man's pockets inside out and take away his savings. The world was to the strong.

Under the stimulus of this the wheels of industry hummed. Factories covered the land. National production grew to a colossal size and the whole outer world seemed laid under a tribute to the great industry. As a system it was far from perfect. It contained in itself all kinds of gross injustices, demands that were too great, wages that were too small; in spite of the splendour of the foreground, poverty and destitution hovered behind the scenes. But such as it was, the system worked: and it was the only one that we knew.

Or turn to another aspect of this same principle of self-help. The way to acquire knowledge in the early days was to buy a tallow candle and read a book after one's day's work, as Benjamin Franklin read or Lincoln: and when the soul was stimulated to it, then the aspiring youth must save money, put himself to college, live on nothing, think much, and in the course of this starvation and effort become a learned man, with somehow a peculiar moral fibre in him not easily reproduced today. For today the candle is free and the college is free and the student has a "Union" like the profiteer's club and a swimming bath and a Drama League and a co-educational society at his elbow for which he buys Beauty Roses at five dollars a bunch.

Or turn if one will to the moral side. The older way of being good was by much prayer and much effort of one's own soul. Now it is done by a Board of Censors. There is no need to fight sin by the power of the spirit: let the Board of Censors do it. They together with three or four kinds of Commissioners are supposed to keep sin at arm's length and to supply a first-class legislative guarantee of righteousness. As a short cut to morality and as a way of saving individual effort our legislatures are turning out morality legislation by the bucketful. The legislature regulates our drink, it begins already to guard us against the deadly cigarette, it regulates here and there the length of our skirts, it safeguards our amusements and in two states of the American Union it even proposes to save us from the teaching of the Darwinian theory of evolution. The ancient prayer "Lead us not into temptation" is passing out of date. The way to temptation is declared closed by Act of Parliament and by amendment to the Constitution of the United States. Yet oddly enough the moral tone of the world fails to respond. The world is apparently more full of thugs, hold-up men, yegg-men, bandits, motor thieves, porch climbers, spotters, spies and crooked policemen than it ever was; till it almost seems that the slow, old-fashioned method of an effort of the individual soul may be needed still before the world is made good.

This vast new system, the system of leaning on the government, is spreading like a blight over England and America, and everywhere we suffer from it. Government, that in theory represents a union of effort and a saving of force, sprawls like an octopus over the land. It has become like a dead weight upon us. Wherever it touches industry it cripples it. It runs railways and makes a heavy deficit : it builds ships and loses money on them : it operates the ships and loses more money : it piles up taxes to fill the vacuum and when it has killed employment, opens a bureau of unemployment and issues a report on the depression of industry.

Now, the only way to restore prosperity is to give back again to the individual the opportunity to make money, to make lots of it, and when he has got it, to keep it. In spite of all the devastation of the war the raw assets of our globe are hardly touched. Here and there, as in parts of China and in England and in Belgium with about seven hundred people to the square mile, the world is fairly well filled up. There is standing room only. But there are vast empty spaces still. Mesopotamia alone has millions of acres of potential wheat land with a few Arabs squatting on it. Canada could absorb easily half a million settlers a year for a generation to come. The most fertile part of the world, the valley of the Amazon, is still untouched: so fertile is it that for tens of thousands of square miles it is choked with trees, a mere tangle of life, defying all entry. The idea of our humanity sadly walking the streets of Glasgow or sitting mournfully fishing on the piers of the Hudson, out of work, would be laughable if it were not for the pathos of it.

The world is out of work for the simple reason that the world has killed the goose that laid the golden eggs of industry. By taxation, by legislation, by popular sentiment all over the world, there has been a disparagement of the capitalist. And all over the world capital is frightened. It goes and hides itself in the form of an investment in a victory bond, a thing that is only a particular name for a debt, with no productive effort behind it and indicating only a dead weight of taxes. There capital sits like a bullfrog hidden behind water lilies, refusing to budge.

Hence the way to restore prosperity is not to multiply government departments and government expenditures, nor to appoint commissions and to pile up debts, but to start going again the machinery of bold productive effort. Take off all the excess profits taxes and the supertaxes on income and as much of the income tax itself as can be done by a wholesale dismissal of government employees and then give industry a mark to shoot at. What is needed now is not the multiplication of government reports, but corporate industry, the formation of land companies, development companies, irrigation companies, any kind of corporation that will call out private capital from its hiding places, offer employment to millions and start the wheels moving again. If the promoters of such corporations presently earn huge fortunes for themselves society is none the worse: and in any case, humanity being what it is, they will hand back a vast part of what they have acquired in return for LL.D. degrees, or bits of blue ribbon, or companionships of the Bath, or whatever kind of glass bead fits the fancy of the retired millionaire.

The next thing to be done, then, is to "fire" the government officials and to bring back the profiteer. As to which officials are to be fired first it doesn't matter much. In England people have been greatly perturbed as to the use to be made of such instruments as the "Geddes Axe": the edge of the axe of dismissal seems so terribly sharp. But there is no need to worry. If the edge of the axe is too sharp, hit with the back of it.

As to the profiteer, bring him back. He is really just the same person who a few years ago was called a Captain of Industry and an Empire Builder and a Nation Maker. It is the times that have changed, not the man. He is there still, just as greedy and rapacious as ever, but no greedier: and we have just the same social need of his greed as a motive power in industry as we ever had, and indeed a worse need than before.

We need him not only in business but in the

whole setting of life, or if not *him* personally, we need the eager, selfish, but reliant spirit of the man who looks after himself and doesn't want to have a spoon-fed education and a government job alternating with a government dole, and a set of morals framed for him by a Board of Censors. Bring back the profiteer: fetch him from the Riviera, from his country place on the Hudson, or from whatever spot to which he has withdrawn with his tin box full of victory bonds. If need be, go and pick him out of the penitentiary, take the stripes off him and tell him to get busy again. Show him the map of the world and ask him to pick out a few likely spots. The trained greed of the rascal will find them in a moment. Then write him out a concession for coal in Asia Minor or oil in the Mackenzie Basin or for irrigation in Mesopotamia. The ink will hardly be dry on it before the capital will begin to flow in: it will come from all kinds of places whence the government could never coax it and where the tax gatherer could never find it. Only promise that it is not going to be taxed out of existence and the stream of capital which is being dried up in the sands of government mismanagement will flow into the hands of private industry like a river of gold.

And incidentally, when the profiteer has finished his work, we can always put him back into the penitentiary if we like. But we need him just now.

IS

COMING TO ENGLAND

?

In the United States and Canada the principal topic of polite conversation is now prohibition. At every dinner party the serving of cocktails immediately introduces the subject: the rest of the dinner is enlivened throughout with the discussion of rum runners, bootleggers, storage of liquor and the State constitution of New Jersey. Under this influence all social and conversational values are shifted and rearranged. A "scholarly" man no longer means a man who can talk well on literary subjects but a man who understands the Eighteenth Amendment and can explain the legal difference between implementing statutes such as the Volstead Act and the underlying state legislation. A "scientist" (invaluable in these conversations) is a man who can make clear the distinction between alcoholic percentages by bulk and by weight. And a "brilliant engineer" means a man who explains how to make home-brewed beer with a kick in it. Similarly, a "raconteur" means a man who has a fund of amusing stories about bootleggers and an "interesting traveller" means a man who has been to Havana and can explain how wet it is. Indeed, the whole conception of travel and of interest in foreign countries is now altered: as soon as anyone mentions that he has been in a foreign country, all the company ask in one breath, "Is it dry?" The question "How is Samoa?" or "How is Turkey?" or "How is British Columbia?" no longer refers to the climate or natural resources: it means "Is the place dry?" When such a question is asked and the answer is "It's wet," there is a deep groan all around the table.

I understand that when the recent disarmament conference met at Washington just as the members were going to sit down at the table Monsieur Briand said to President Harding, "How dry is the United States, anyway?" And the whole assembly talked about it for half an hour. That was why the first newspaper bulletins merely said, "Conference exchanges credentials."

As a discoverer of England I therefore made it one of my chief cares to try to obtain accurate information of this topic. I was well aware that immediately on my return to Canada the first question I would be asked would be "Is England going dry?" I realized that in any report I might make to the National Geographical Society or to the Political Science Association, the members of these bodies, being scholars, would want accurate information about the price of whisky, the percentage of alcohol, and the hours of opening and closing the saloons.

My first impression on the subject was, I must say, one of severe moral shock. Landing in England after spending the summer in Ontario, it seemed a terrible thing to see people openly drinking on an English train. On an Ontario train, as everybody knows, there is no way of taking a drink except by climbing up on the roof, lying flat on one's stomach, and taking a suck out of a flask. But in England in any dining car one actually sees a waiter approach a person dining and say, "Beer, sir, or wine?" This is done in broad daylight with no apparent sense of criminality or moral shame. Appalling though it sounds, bottled ale is openly sold on the trains at twenty-five cents a bottle and dry sherry at eighteen cents a glass.

When I first saw this I expected to see the waiter arrested on the spot. I looked around to see if there were any "spotters," detectives, or secret service men on the train. I anticipated that the train conductor would appear and throw the waiter off the car. But then I realized that I was in England and that in the British Isles they still tolerate the consumption of alcohol. Indeed, I doubt if they are even aware that they are "consuming alcohol." Their impression is that they are drinking beer.

At the beginning of my discussion I will therefore preface a few exact facts and statistics for the use of geographical societies, learned bodies and government commissions. The quantity of beer consumed in England in a given period is about 200,000,000 gallons. The life of a bottle of Scotch whisky is seven seconds. The number of public houses, or "pubs," in the English countryside is one to every half mile. The percentage of the working classes drinking beer is 125: the percentage of the class without work drinking beer is 200.

Statistics like these do not, however, give a final answer to the question, "Is prohibition coming to England?" They merely show that it is not there now. The question itself will be answered in as many different ways as there are different kinds of people. Any prohibitionist will tell you that the coming of prohibition to England is as certain as the coming eclipse of the sun. But this is always so. It is in human nature that people are impressed by the cause they work in. I once knew a minister of the Scotch Church who took a voyage round the world: he said that the thing that impressed him most was the growth of Presbyterianism in Japan. No doubt it did. When the Orillia lacrosse team took their trip to Australia, they said on their return that lacrosse was spreading all over the world. In the same way there is said to be a spread all over the world of Christian Science, proportional representation, militarism, peace sentiment, barbarism, altruism, psychoanalysis and death from wood alcohol. They are what are called world movements.

My own judgement in regard to prohibition in the British Isles is this: In Scotland, prohibition is not coming: if anything, it is going. In Ireland, prohibition will only be introduced when they have run out of other forms of trouble. But in England I think that prohibition could easily come unless the English people realize where they are drifting and turn back. They are in the early stage of the movement already.

Turning first to Scotland, there is no fear, I say, that prohibition will be adopted there: and this from the simple reason that the Scotch do not drink. I have elsewhere alluded to the extraordinary misapprehension that exists in regard to the Scotch people and their sense of humour. I find a similar popular error in regard to the use of whisky by the Scotch. Because they manufacture the best whisky in the world, the Scotch, in popular fancy, are often thought to be addicted to the drinking of it. This is purely a delusion. During the whole of two or three pleasant weeks spent in lecturing in Scotland, I never on any occasion saw whisky made use of *as a beverage*. I have seen people take it, of course, as a medicine, or as a precaution, or as a wise offset against a rather treacherous climate; but as a beverage, never.

The manner and circumstance of their offering whisky to a stranger amply illustrates their point of view towards it. Thus at my first lecture in Glasgow where I was to appear before a large and fashionable audience, the chairman said to me in the committee room that he was afraid that there might be a draught on the platform. Here was a serious matter. For a lecturer who has to earn his living by his occupation, a draught on the platform is not a thing to be disregarded. It might kill him. Nor is it altogether safe for the chairman himself, a man already in middle life, to be exposed to a current of cold air. In this case, therefore, the chairman suggested that he thought it might be "prudent" —that was his word, "prudent"—if I should take a small drop of whisky before encountering the draught. In return I told him that I could not think of his accompanying me to the platform unless he would let me insist on his taking a very reasonable precaution. Whisky taken on these terms not only seems like a duty but it tastes better.

In the same way I find that in Scotland it is very often necessary to take something to drink on purely meteorological grounds. The weather simply cannot be trusted. A man might find that on "going out into the weather" he is overwhelmed by a heavy fog or an avalanche of snow or a driving storm of rain. In such a case a mere drop of whisky might save his life. It would be folly not to take it. Again—"coming in out of the weather" is a thing not to be trifled with. A person coming in unprepared and unprotected might be seized with angina pectoris or appendicitis and die upon the spot. No reasonable person would refuse the simple precaution of taking a small drop immediately after his entry.

I find that, classified altogether, there are seventeen reasons advanced in Scotland for taking whisky. They run as follows: Reason one, because it is raining; Two, because it is not raining; Three, because you are just going out into the weather; Four, because you have just come in from the weather; Five—no, I forget the ones that come after that. But I remember that reason number seventeen is "because it canna do ye any harm." On the whole, reason seventeen is the best.

Put in other words this means that the Scotch make use of whisky with dignity and without shame: and they never call it alcohol.

In England the case is different. Already the English are showing the first signs that indicate the possible approach of prohibition. Already all over England there are weird regulations about the closing hours of the public houses. They open and close according to the varying regulations of the municipality. In some places they open at six in the morning, close down for an hour from nine till ten, open then till noon, shut for ten minutes, and so on; in some places they are open in the morning and closed in the evening; in other places they are open in the evening and closed in the morning. The ancient idea was that a wayside public house was a place of sustenance and comfort, a human need that might be wanted any hour. It was in the same class with the lifeboat or the emergency ambulance. Under the old common law the innkeeper must supply meat and drink at any hour. If he was asleep the traveller might wake him. And in those days meat and drink were regarded in the same light. Note how great the change is. In modern life in England there is nothing that you dare wake up a man for except gasoline. The mere fact that you need a drink is no longer held to entitle you to break his rest.

In London especially one feels the full force of the "closing" regulations. The bars open and shut at intervals like daisies blinking at the sun. And like the flowers at evening they close their petals with the darkness. In London they have already adopted the deadly phrases of the prohibitionist, such as "alcohol" and "liquor traffic" and so on: and already the "sale of spirits" stops absolutely at about eleven o'clock at night.

This means that after theatre hours London is a "city of dreadful night." The people from the theatre scuttle to their homes. The lights are extinguished in the windows. The streets darken. Only a belated taxi still moves. At midnight the place is deserted. At I A.M., the lingering footfalls echo in the empty street. Here and there a restaurant in a fashionable street makes a poor pretence of keeping open for after-theatre suppers. Odd people, the shivering wrecks of theatre parties, are huddled here and there. A gloomy waiter lays a sardine on the table. The guests charge their glasses with Perrier water, lithia water, citrate of magnesia, or Bromo Seltzer. They eat the sardine and vanish into the night. Not even Oshkosh, Wisconsin, or Middlebury, Vermont, is quieter than is the night life of London. It may no doubt seem a wise thing to go to bed early. But it is a terrible thing to go to bed early by Act of Parliament.

All of which means that the people of England are not facing the prohibition question fairly and squarely. If they see no harm in "consuming alcohol" they ought to say so and let their code of regulations reflect the fact. But the "closing" and "regulating" and "squeezing" of the "liquor traffic," without any outspoken protest, means letting the whole case go by default. Under these circumstances an organized and active minority can always win and impose its will upon the crowd.

When I was in England I amused myself one day by writing an imaginary picture of what England will be like when the last stage is reached and London goes the way of New York and Chicago. I cast it in the form of a letter from an American prohibitionist in which he describes the final triumph of prohibition in England. With the permission of the reader I reproduce it here:

THE ADVENT OF PROHIBITION IN ENGLAND
*As written in the correspondence of
an American visitor*

How glad I am that I have lived to see this wonderful reform of prohibition at last accomplished in England. There is something so difficult about the British, so stolid, so hard to move.

We tried everything in the great campaign that we made, and for ever so long it didn't seem to work. We had processions, just as we did at home in America, with great banners carried round bearing the inscription: "Do you want to save the boy?" But these people looked on and said, "Boy? Boy? What boy?" Our workers were almost disheartened. "Oh, sir," said one of them, an ex-barkeeper from Oklahoma, "it does seem so hard that we have total prohibition in the States and here they can get all the drink they want." And the good fellow broke down and sobbed.

But at last it has come. After the most terrific efforts we managed to get this nation stampeded, and for more than a month now England has been dry. I wish you could have witnessed the scenes, just like what we saw at home in America, when it was known that the bill had passed. The members of the House of Lords all stood up on their seats and yelled, "Rah! Rah! Rah! Who's bone dry? We are!" And the brewers and innkeepers were emptying their barrels of beer into the Thames just as at St Louis they emptied the beer into the Mississippi.

I can't tell you with what pleasure I watched a group of members of the Athenaeum Club sitting on the bank of the Thames and opening bottles of champagne and pouring them into the river. "To think," said one of them to me, "that there was a time when I used to lap up a couple of quarts of this terrible stuff every evening." I got him to give me a few bottles as a souvenir, and I got some more souvenirs, whisky and liqueurs, when the members of the Beafsteak Club were emptying out their cellars into Green Street; so when you come over, I shall still be able, of course, to give you a drink.

We have, as I said, been bone dry only a month, and yet already we are getting the same splendid results as in America. All the big dinners are now as refined and as elevating and the dinner speeches as long and as informal as they are in New York or Toronto. The other night at a dinner at the White Friars Club I heard Sir Owen Seaman speaking, not in that light futile way that he used to have, but quite differently. He talked for over an hour and a half on the State ownership of the Chinese railway system, and I almost fancied myself back in Boston.

And the working class too. It is just wonderful how prohibition has increased their efficiency. In the old days they used to drop their work the moment the hour struck. Now they simply refuse to do so. I noticed yesterday a foreman in charge of a building operation vainly trying to call the bricklayers down. "Come, come, gentlemen," he shouted, "I must insist on your stopping for the night." But they just went on laying bricks faster than ever.

Of course, as yet there are a few slight difficulties and deficiencies, just as there are with us in America. We have had the same trouble with wood alcohol (they call it methylated spirit here), with the same deplorable results. On some days the list of deaths is very serious, and in some cases we are losing men we can hardly spare. A great many of our leading actors —in fact, most of them—are dead. And there has been a heavy loss, too, among the literary class and in the legal profession.

There was a very painful scene last week at the dinner of the Benchers of Gray's Inn. It seems that one of the chief justices had undertaken to make home brew for the Benchers, just as the people do on our side of the water. He got one of the waiters to fetch him some hops and three raw potatoes, a packet of yeast and some boiling water. In the end, four of the Benchers were carried out dead. But they are going to give them a public funeral in the Abbey.

I regret to say that the death list in the Royal Navy is very heavy. Some of the best sailors are gone, and it is very difficult to keep admirals. But I have tried to explain to the people here that these are merely the things that one must expect, and that, with a little patience, they will have bone-dry admirals and bone-dry statesmen just as good as the wet ones. Even the clergy can be dried up with firmness and perseverance.

There was also a slight sensation here when the Chancellor of the Exchequer brought in his first appropriation for maintaining prohibition. From our point of view in America, it was modest enough. But these people are not used to it. The Chancellor merely asked for ten million pounds a month to begin on; he explained that his task was heavy; he has to police, not only the entire coast, but also the interior; for the Grampian Hills of Scotland alone he asked a million. There was a good deal of questioning in the House over these figures. The Chancellor was asked if he intended to keep a hired spy at every street corner in London. He answered, "No, only on every other street." He added also that every spy must wear a brass collar with his number.

I must admit further, and I am sorry to have to tell you this, that now we have prohibition it is becoming increasingly difficult to get a drink. In fact, sometimes, especially in the very early morning, it is most inconvenient and almost impossible. The public houses being closed, it is necessary to go into a drug store—just as it is with us—and lean up against the counter and make a gurgling sound like apoplexy. One often sees these apoplexy cases lined up four deep.

But the people are finding substitutes, just as they do with us. There is a tremendous run on patent medicines, perfume, glue and nitric acid. It has been found that Shear's soap contains alcohol, and one sees people everywhere eating cakes of it. The upper classes have taken to chewing tobacco very considerably, and the use of opium in the House of Lords has very greatly increased.

But I don't want you to think that if you come over here to see me, your private life will be in any way impaired or curtailed. I am glad to say that I have plenty of rich connections whose cellars are very amply stocked. The Duke of Blank is said to have

5,000 cases of Scotch whisky, and I have managed to get a card of introduction to his butler. In fact you will find that, just as with us in America, the benefit of prohibition is intended to fall on the poorer classes. There is no desire to interfere with the rich.

WE

HAVE

WITH

US

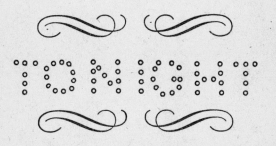

TONIGHT

Not only during my tour in England but for many years past it has been my lot to speak and to lecture in all sorts of places, under all sorts of circumstances and before all sorts of audiences. I say this, not in boastfulness, but in sorrow. Indeed, I only mention it to establish the fact that when I talk of lecturers and speakers, I talk of what I know.

Few people realize how arduous and how disagreeable public lecturing is. The public sees the lecturer step out on to the platform in his little white waistcoat and his long tailed coat and with a false air of a conjurer about him, and they think him happy. After about ten minutes of his talk they are tired of him. Most people tire of a lecture in ten minutes; clever people can do it in five. Sensible people never go to lectures at all. But the people who do go to a lecture and who get tired of it, presently hold it as a sort of a grudge against the lecturer personally. In reality his sufferings are worse than theirs.

For my own part I always try to appear as happy as possible while I am lecturing. I take this to be part of the trade of anybody labelled a humorist and paid as such. I have no sympathy whatever with the idea that a humorist ought to be a lugubrious person with a face stamped with melancholy. This is a cheap and elementary effect belonging to the level of a circus clown. The image of "laughter shaking both his sides" is the truer picture of comedy. Therefore, I say, I always try to appear cheerful at my lectures and even to laugh at my own jokes. Oddly enough this arouses a kind of resentment in some of the audience. "Well, I will say," said a stern-looking woman who spoke to me after one of my lectures, "you certainly do seem to enjoy your own fun." "Madam," I answered, "if I didn't, who would?" But in reality the whole business of being a public lecturer is one long variation of boredom and fatigue. So I propose to set down here some of the many trials which the lecturer has to bear.

The first of the troubles which anyone who begins giving public lectures meets at the very outset is the fact that the audience won't come to hear him. This happens invariably and constantly, and not through any fault or shortcoming of the speaker.

I don't say that this happened very often to me in my tour in England. In nearly all cases I had crowded audiences: by dividing up the money that I received by the average number of people present to hear me I have calculated that they paid thirteen cents each. And my lectures are evidently worth thirteen cents. But at home in Canada I have very often tried the fatal experiment of lecturing for nothing: and in that case the audience simply won't come. A man will turn out at night when he knows he is going to hear a first-class thirteen cent lecture; but when the thing is given for nothing, why go to it?

The city in which I live is overrun with little societies, clubs and associations, always wanting to be addressed. So at least it is in appearance. In reality the societies are composed of presidents, secretaries and officials, who want the conspicuousness of office, and a large list of other members who won't come to the meetings. For such an association, the invited speaker who is to lecture for nothing prepares his lecture on "Indo-Germanic Factors in the Current of History." If he is a professor, he takes all the winter at it. You may drop in at his house at any time and his wife will tell you that he is "upstairs working on his lecture." If he comes down at all it is in carpet slippers and dressing gown. His mental vision of his meeting is that of a huge gathering of keen people with Indo-Germanic faces, hanging upon every word.

Then comes the fated night. There are seventeen people present. The lecturer refuses to count them. He refers to them afterwards as "about a hundred." To this group he reads his paper on the Indo-Germanic Factor. It takes him two hours. When he is over the chairman invites discussion. There is *no* discussion. The audience is willing to let the Indo-Germanic factors go unchallenged. Then the chairman makes this speech. He says:

"I am very sorry indeed that we should have had such a very poor turn-out tonight. I am sure that the members who were not here have missed a real treat in the delightful paper that we have listened to. I want to assure the lecturer that if he comes to the Owls' Club again we can guarantee him next time a capacity audience. And will any members, please, who haven't paid their dollar this winter, pay it either to me or to Mr Sibley as they pass out."

I have heard this speech (in the years when I

have had to listen to it) so many times that I know it by heart. I have made the acquaintance of the Owls' Club under so many names that I recognize it at once. I am aware that its members refuse to turn out in cold weather; that they do not turn out in wet weather; that when the weather is really fine, it is impossible to get them together; that the slightest counter-attraction—a hockey match, a sacred concert—goes to their heads at once.

There was a time when I was the newly appointed occupant of a college chair and had to address the Owls' Club. It is a penalty that all new professors pay; and the Owls batten upon them like bats. It is one of the compensations of age that I am free of the Owls' Club forever. But in the days when I still had to address them, I used to take it out of the Owls in a speech, delivered, in imagination only and not out loud, to the assembled meeting of the seventeen Owls, after the chairman had made his concluding remarks. It ran as follows:

"Gentlemen—if you are such, which I doubt. I realize that the paper which I have read on 'Was Hegel a deist?' has been an error. I spent all the winter on it and now I realize that not one of you pups know who Hegel was or what a deist is. Never mind. It is over now, and I am glad. But just let me say this, only this, which won't keep you a minute. Your chairman has been good enough to say that if I come again you will get together a capacity audience to hear me. Let me tell you that if your society waits for its next meeting till I come to address you again, you will wait indeed. In fact, gentlemen—I say it very frankly—it will be in another world."

But I pass over the audience. Suppose there is a real audience, and suppose them all duly gathered together. Then it becomes the business of that gloomy gentleman—facetiously referred to in the newspaper reports as the "genial chairman"—to put the lecturer to the bad. In nine cases out of ten he can do so. Some chairmen, indeed, develop a great gift for it. Here are one or two examples from my own experience :

"Ladies and gentlemen," said the chairman of a society in a little country town in Western Ontario, to which I had come as a paid (a very humbly paid) lecturer, "we have with us tonight a gentleman" (here he made an attempt to read my name on a card, failed to read it and put the card back in his pocket)—"a gentleman who is to lecture to us on" (here he looked at his card again)—"on Ancient—Ancient—I don't very well see what it is—Ancient—Britain? Thank you, on Ancient Britain. Now, this is the first of our series of lectures for this winter. The last series, as you all know, was not a success. In fact, we came out at the end of the year with a deficit. So this year we are starting a new line and trying the experiment of cheaper talent."

Here the chairman gracefully waved his hand toward me and there was a certain amount of applause. "Before I sit down," the chairman added, "I'd like to say that I am sorry to see such a poor turn-out tonight and to ask any of the members who haven't paid their dollar to pay it either to me or to Mr Sibley as they pass out."

Let anybody who knows the discomfiture of coming out before an audience on any terms, judge how it feels to crawl out in front of them labelled *cheaper talent*.

Another charming way in which the chairman endeavours to put both the speaker for the evening and the audience into an entirely good humour, is by reading out letters of regret from persons unable to be present. This, of course, is only for grand occasions when the speaker has been invited to come under very special auspices. It was my fate, not long ago, to "appear" (this is the correct word to use in this connection) in this capacity when I was going about Canada trying to raise some money for the relief of the Belgians. I travelled in great glory with a pass on the Canadian Pacific Railway (not since extended : officials of the road kindly note this) and was most generously entertained wherever I went.

It was, therefore, the business of the chairman at such meetings as these to try and put a special distinction or cachet on the gathering. This is how it was done :

"Ladies and gentlemen," said the chairman, rising from his seat on the platform with a little bundle of papers in his hand, "before I introduce the speaker of the evening, I have one or two items that I want to read to you." Here he rustles his papers and there is a deep hush in the hall while he selects one. "We had hoped to have with us tonight Sir Robert Borden, the Prime Minister of this Dominion. I have just received a telegram from Sir Robert in which he says that he will not be able to be here" (*great applause*). The chairman puts up his hand for silence, picks up another telegram and continues. "Our committee, ladies and gentlemen, telegraphed an invitation to Sir Wilfrid Laurier very cordially inviting him to be here tonight. I have here Sir Wilfrid's answer in which he says that he will not be able to be with us" (*renewed applause*). The chairman again puts up his hand for silence and goes on, picking up one paper after another. "The Minister of Finance regrets that he will be unable to come" (*applause*). "Mr Rodolphe Lemieux (*applause*) will not be here (*great applause*)—the Mayor of Toronto (*applause*) is detained on business (*wild applause*)—the Anglican Bishop of the Diocese (*applause*)—the Principal of the University College, Toronto (*great applause*)—the Minister of Education (*applause*)—none of these are coming." There is a great clapping of hands and enthusiasm, after which the meeting is called to order with a very distinct and palpable feeling that it is one of the most distinguished audiences ever gathered in the hall.

Here is another experience of the same period while I was pursuing the same exalted purpose : I arrived in a little town in Eastern Ontario, and found to my horror that I was billed to "appear" *in a church*. I was supposed to give readings from my works, and my books are supposed to be of a humorous character. A church hardly seemed the right place to get funny in. I explained my difficulty to the pastor of the church, a very solemn-looking man. He nodded his head, slowly and gravely, as he grasped my difficulty. "I see," he said, "I see, but I think that I can introduce you to our people in such a way as to make that right."

When the time came, he led me up on to the pulpit platform of the church, just beside and below the pulpit itself, with a reading desk and a big Bible and a shaded light beside it. It was a big church, and the audience, sitting in half darkness, as is customary during a sermon, reached away back into the gloom. The place was packed full and absolutely quiet. Then the chairman spoke:

"Dear friends," he said, "I want you to understand that it will be all right to laugh tonight. Let me hear you laugh heartily, laugh right out, just as much as ever you want to, because—" (and here his voice assumed the deep sepulchral tones of the preacher)— "when we think of the noble object for which the professor appears tonight, we may be assured that the Lord will forgive anyone who will laugh at the professor."

I am sorry to say, however, that none of the audience, even with the plenary absolution in advance, were inclined to take a chance on it.

I recall in this same connection the chairman of a meeting at a certain town in Vermont. He represents the type of chairman who turns up so late in the evening that the committee have no time to explain to him properly what the meeting is about or who the speaker is. I noticed on this occasion that he introduced me very guardedly by name (from a little card) and said nothing about the Belgians, and nothing about my being (supposed to be) a humorist. This last was a great error. The audience, for want of guidance, remained very silent and decorous, and well behaved during my talk. Then, somehow, at the end, while someone was moving a vote of thanks, the chairman discovered his error. So he tried to make it good. Just as the audience were getting up to put on their wraps, he rose, knocked on his desk and said :

"Just a minute, please, ladies and gentlemen, just a minute. I have just found out—I should have known it sooner, but I was late in coming to this meeting—that the speaker who has just addressed you has done so in behalf of the Belgian Relief Fund. I understand that he is a well-known Canadian humorist (ha! ha!) and I am sure that we have all been immensely amused (ha! ha!). He is giving his delightful talks (ha! ha!)—though I didn't know this till just this minute—for the Belgian Relief Fund, and he is giving his services for nothing. I am sure when we realize this, we shall all feel that it has been well worth while to come. I am only sorry that we didn't have a better turn-out tonight. But I can assure the speaker that if he will come again, we shall guarantee him a capacity audience. And I may say, that if there are any members of this association who have not paid their dollar this season, they can give it either to myself or to Mr Sibley as they pass out."

With the amount of accumulated experience that I had behind me I was naturally interested during my lecture in England in the chairmen who were to introduce me. I cannot help but feel that I have acquired a fine taste in chairmen. I know them just as other experts know old furniture and Pekinese dogs. The witty chairman, the prosy chairman, the solemn chairman—I know them all. As soon as I shake hands with the chairman in the committee room I can tell exactly how he will act.

There are certain types of chairmen who have so often been described and are so familiar that it is not worth while to linger on them. Everybody knows the chairman who says, "Now, ladies and gentlemen, you have not come here to listen to *me*. So I will be very brief; in fact, I will confine my remarks to just one or two very short observations." He then proceeds to make observations for twenty-five minutes. At the end of it he remarks with charming simplicity, "Now I know that you are all impatient to hear the lecturer ..."

And everybody knows the chairman who comes to the meeting with a very imperfect knowledge of who or what the lecturer is, and is driven to introduce him by saying:

"Our lecturer of the evening is widely recognized as one of the greatest authorities on—on—on his subject in the world today. He comes to us from—from a great distance and I can assure him that it is a great pleasure to this audience to welcome a man who has done so much to—to—to advance the interests of—of—of everything as he has."

But this man, bad as he is, is not so bad as the chairman whose preparation for introducing the speaker has obviously been made at the eleventh hour. Just such a chairman it was my fate to strike in the form of a local alderman, built like an ox, in one of those small manufacturing places in the north of England where they grow men of this type and elect them into office.

"I never saw the lecturer before," he said, "but I've read his book." (I have written nineteen books.) "The committee was good enough to send me over his book last night. I didn't read it all but I took a look at the preface and I can assure him that he is very welcome. I understand he comes from a college. . . ." Then he turned directly towards me and said in a loud voice, "What was the name of that college over there you said you came from?"

"McGill," I answered equally loudly.

"He comes from McGill," the chairman boomed out. "I never heard of McGill myself but I can assure him he's welcome. He's going to lecture us on— what did you say it was to be about?"

"It's a humorous lecture," I said.

"Ay, it's to be a humorous lecture, ladies and gentlemen, and I'll venture to say it will be a rare treat. I'm only sorry I can't stay for it myself as I have to get back over to the Town Hall for a meeting. So without more ado I'll get off the platform and let the lecturer go on with his humour."

A still more terrible type of chairman is one whose mind is evidently preoccupied and disturbed with some local happening and who comes on to the platform with a face imprinted with distress. Before introducing the lecturer he refers in moving tones to the local sorrow, whatever it is. As a prelude to a humorous lecture this is not gay.

Such a chairman fell to my lot one night before a gloomy audience in a London suburb.

"As I look about this hall tonight," he began in a doleful whine, "I see many empty seats." Here he stifled a sob. "Nor am I surprised that a great many of our people should prefer tonight to stay quietly at home—"

I had no clue to what he meant. I merely gathered that some particular sorrow must have overwhelmed the town that day.

"To many it may seem hardly fitting that after the loss our town has sustained we should come out here to listen to a humorous lecture—"

"What's the trouble?" I whispered to a citizen sitting beside me on the platform.

"Our oldest resident—" he whispered back—"he died this morning."

"How old?"

"Ninety-four," he whispered.

Meantime the chairman, with deep sobs in his voice, continued :

"We debated in our committee whether or not we should have the lecture. Had it been a lecture of another character our position would have been less difficult—"

By this time I began to feel like a criminal.

"The case would have been different had the lecture been one that contained information, or that was inspired by some serious purpose, or that could have been of any benefit. But this is not so. We understand that this lecture which Mr Leacock has already given, I believe, twenty or thirty times in England—"

Here he turned to me with a look of mild reproof while the silent audience, deeply moved, all looked at me as at a man who went round the country insulting the memory of the dead by giving a lecture thirty times.

"We understand, though this we shall have an opportunity of testing for ourselves presently, that Mr Leacock's lecture is not of a character which—has not, so to speak, the kind of value—in short, is not a lecture of that class."

Here he paused and choked back a sob.

"Had our poor friend been spared to us for another six years he would have rounded out the century. But it was not to be. For two or three years past he had noted that somehow his strength was failing, that, for some reason or other, he was no longer what he had been. Last month he began to droop. Last week he began to sink. Speech left him last Tuesday. This morning he passed, and he has gone now, we trust, in safety to where there are no lectures."

The audience were now nearly in tears.

The chairman made a visible effort towards firmness and control.

"But yet," he continued, "our committee felt that in another sense it was our duty to go on with our arrangements. I think, ladies and gentlemen, that the war has taught us all that it is always our duty to 'carry on,' no matter how hard it may be, no matter with what reluctance we do it, and whatever be the difficulties and the dangers, we must carry on to the end: for after all there is an end and by resolution and patience we can reach it.

"I will, therefore, invite Mr Leacock to deliver to us his humorous lecture, the title of which I have forgotten, but I understand it to be the same lecture which he has already given thirty or forty times in England."

But contrast with this melancholy man the genial and pleasing person who introduced me, all upside down, to a metropolitan audience.

He was so brisk, so neat, so sure of himself that it didn't seem possible that he could make any kind of mistake. I thought it unnecessary to coach him. He seemed absolutely all right.

"It is a great pleasure," he said, with a charming, easy appearance of being entirely at home on the platform, "to welcome here tonight our distinguished Canadian fellow citizen, Mr Learoyd—" he turned halfway towards me as he spoke with a sort of gesture of welcome, admirably executed. If only my name had been Learoyd instead of Leacock it would have been excellent.

"There are many of us," he continued, "who have awaited Mr Learoyd's coming with the most pleasant anticipations. We seemed from his books to know him already as an old friend. In fact I think I do not exaggerate when I tell Mr Learoyd that his name in our city has long been a household word. I have very, very great pleasure, ladies and gentlemen, in introducing to you Mr Learoyd."

As far as I know that chairman never knew his error. At the close of my lecture he said that he was sure that the audience "were deeply indebted to Mr Learoyd," and then with a few words of rapid, genial apology buzzed off, like a humming bird, to other avocations. But I have amply forgiven him: anything for kindness and geniality; it makes the whole of life smooth. If that chairman ever comes to my home town he is hereby invited to lunch or dine with me, as Mr Learoyd or under any name that he selects.

Such a man is, after all, in sharp contrast to the kind of chairman who has no native sense of the geniality that ought to accompany his office. There is, for example, a type of man who thinks that the fitting way to introduce a lecturer is to say a few words about the finances of the society to which he is to lecture (for money) and about the difficulty of getting members to turn out to hear lectures.

Everybody has heard such a speech a dozen times. But it is the paid lecturer sitting on the platform who best appreciates it. It runs like this:

"Now, ladies and gentlemen, before I invite the lecturer of the evening to address us there are a few words that I would like to say. There are a good many members who are in arrears with their fees. I am aware that these are hard times and it is difficult to collect money but at the same time the members ought to remember that the expenses of the society are very heavy. The fees that are asked by the lecturers, as I suppose you know, have advanced very greatly in the last few years.

In fact I may say that they are becoming almost prohibitive."

This discourse is pleasant hearing for the lecturer. He can see the members who have not yet paid their annual dues eyeing him with hatred. The chairman goes on:

"Our finance committee were afraid at first that we could not afford to bring Mr Leacock to our society. But fortunately through the personal generosity of two of our members who subscribed ten pounds each out of their own pocket we are able to raise the required sum."

(*Applause: during which the lecturer sits looking and feeling like the embodiment of the "required sum."*)

"Now, ladies and gentlemen," continues the chairman, "what I feel is that when we have members in the society who are willing to make this sacrifice—because it is a sacrifice, ladies and gentlemen—we ought to support them in every way. The members ought to think it their duty to turn out to the lectures. I know that it is not an easy thing to do. On a cold night, like this evening, it is hard, I admit it is hard, to turn out from the comfort of one's own fireside and come and listen to a lecture. But I think that the members should look at it not as a matter of personal comfort but as a matter of duty towards this society. We have managed to keep this society alive for fifteen years and, though I don't say it in any spirit of boasting, it has not been an easy thing to do. It has required a good deal of pretty hard spade work by the committee. Well, ladies and gentlemen, I suppose you didn't come here to listen to me and perhaps I have said enough about our difficulties and troubles. So without more ado—" (this is always a favourite phrase with chairmen)—"I'll invite Mr Leacock to address the society—oh, just a word before I sit down. Will all those who are leaving before the end of the lecture kindly go out through the side door and step as quietly as possible? Mr Leacock."

Anybody who is in the lecture business knows that that introduction is far worse than being called Mr Learoyd.

When any lecturer goes across to England from this side of the water there is naturally a tendency on the part of the chairman to play upon this fact. This is especially true in the case of a Canadian like myself. The chairman feels that the moment is fitting for one of those great imperial thoughts that bind the British Empire together. But sometimes the expression of the thought falls short of the full glory of the conception.

Witness this (word for word) introduction that was used against me by a clerical chairman in a quiet spot in the south of England:

"Not so long ago, ladies and gentlemen," said the vicar, "we used to send out to Canada various classes of our community to help build up that country. We sent out our labourers, we sent out our scholars and professors. Indeed we even sent out our criminals. And now," with a wave of his hand towards me, "they are coming back."

There was no laughter. An English audience is nothing if not literal; and they are as polite as they are literal. They understood that I was a reformed criminal and as such they gave me a hearty burst of applause.

But there is just one thing that I would like to chronicle here in favour of the chairman and in gratitude for his assistance. Even at his worst he is far better than having no chairman at all. Over in England a great many societies and public bodies have adopted the plan of "cutting out the chairman." Wearying of his faults, they have forgotten the reasons for his existence and undertaken to do without him.

The result is ghastly. The lecturer steps up on to the platform alone and unaccompanied. There is a feeble ripple of applause; he makes his miserable bow and explains with as much enthusiasm as he can who he is. The atmosphere of the thing is so cold that an Arctic expedition isn't in it. I found also the further difficulty that in the absence of the chairman very often the audience, or a large part of it, doesn't know who the lecturer is. On many occasions I received on appearing a wild burst of applause under the impression that I was somebody else. I have been mistaken in this way for Mr Briand, then Prime Minister of France, for Charlie Chaplin, for Mrs Asquith—but stop, I may get into a libel suit. All I mean is that without a chairman "we celebrities" get terribly mixed up together.

To one experience of my tour as a lecturer I shall always be able to look back with satisfaction. I nearly had the pleasure of killing a man with laughing: and this in the most literal sense. American lecturers have often dreamed of doing this. I nearly did it. The man in question was a comfortable apoplectic-looking man with the kind of merry rubicund face that is seen in countries where they don't have prohibition. He was seated near the back of the hall and was laughing uproariously. All of a sudden I realized that something was happening. The man had collapsed sideways on to the floor; a little group of men gathered about him; they lifted him up and I could see them carrying him out, a silent and inert mass. As in duty bound I went right on with my lecture. But my heart beat high with satisfaction. I was sure that I had killed him. The reader may judge how high these hopes rose when a moment or two later a note was handed to the chairman who then asked me to pause for a moment in my lecture and stood up and asked, "Is there a doctor in the audience?" A doctor rose and silently went out. The lecture continued; but there was no more laughter; my aim had now become to kill another of them and they knew it. They were aware that if they started laughing they might die. In a few minutes a second note was handed to the chairman. He announced very gravely, "A second doctor is wanted." The lecture went on in deeper silence than ever. All the audience were waiting for a third announcement. It came. A new message was handed to the chairman. He rose and said, "If Mr Murchison, the undertaker, is in the audience, will he kindly step outside."

That man, I regret to say, got well. Disappointing though it is to read it, he recovered. I sent back next morning from London a telegram of inquiry (I did it in reality so as to have a proper proof of his death) and received the answer, "Patient doing well; is sitting up in bed and reading Lord Haldane's *Relativity*; no danger of relapse."

HAVE
THE
ENGLISH
ANY
SENSE
OF
HUMOUR
?

It was understood that the main object of my trip to England was to find out whether the British people have any sense of humour. No doubt the Geographical Society had this investigation in mind in not paying my expenses. Certainly on my return I was at once assailed with the question on all sides, "Have they got a sense of humour? Even if it is only a rudimentary sense, have they got it or have they not?" I propose therefore to address myself to the answer to this question.

A peculiar interest always attaches to humour. There is no quality of the human mind about which its possessor is more sensitive than the sense of humour. A man will freely confess that he has no ear for music, or no taste for fiction, or even no interest in religion. But

I have yet to see the man who announces that he has no sense of humour. In point of fact, every man is apt to think himself possessed of an exceptional gift in this direction, and that even if his humour does not express itself in the power either to make a joke or to laugh at one, it none the less consists in a peculiar insight or inner light superior to that of other people.

The same thing is true of nations. Each thinks its own humour of an entirely superior kind, and either refuses to admit, or admits reluctantly, the humorous quality of other peoples. The Englishman may credit the Frenchman with a certain light effervescence of mind which he neither emulates nor envies; the Frenchman may acknowledge that English literature shows here and there a sort of heavy playfulness; but neither of them would consider that the humour of the other nation could stand a moment's comparison with his own.

Yet, oddly enough, American humour stands as a conspicuous exception to this general rule. A certain vogue clings to it. Ever since the spacious days of Artemus Ward and Mark Twain it has enjoyed an extraordinary reputation, and this not only on our own continent, but in England. It was in a sense the English who "discovered" Mark Twain; I mean it was they who first clearly recognized him as a man of letters of the foremost rank, at a time when academic Boston still tried to explain him away as a mere comic man of the West. In the same way Artemus Ward is still held in affectionate remembrance in London, and, of the later generation, Mr Dooley at least is a household word.

This is so much the case that a sort of legend has grown around American humour. It is presumed to be a superior article and to enjoy the same kind of pre-eminence as French cooking, the Russian ballet, and Italian organ grinding. With this goes the converse supposition that the British people are inferior in humour, that a joke reaches them only with great difficulty, and that a British audience listens to humour in gloomy and unintelligent silence. People still love to repeat the famous story of how John Bright listened attentively to Artemus Ward's lecture in London and then said, gravely, that he "doubted many of the young man's statements"; and readers still remember Mark Twain's famous parody of the discussion of his book by a wooden-headed reviewer of an English review.

But the legend in reality is only a legend. If the English are inferior to Americans in humour, I, for one, am at a loss to see where it comes in. If there is anything on our continent superior in humour to *Punch* I should like to see it. If we have any more humorous writers in our midst than E. V. Lucas and Charles Graves and Owen Seaman I should like to read what they write; and if there is any audience capable of more laughter and more generous appreciation than an audience in London, or Bristol, or Aberdeen, I should like to lecture to it.

During my voyage of discovery in Great Britain I had very exceptional opportunities for testing the truth of these comparisons. It was my good fortune to appear as an avowed humorist in all the great British cities. I lectured as far north as Aberdeen and as far south as Brighton and Bournemouth; I travelled eastward to Ipswich and westward into Wales. I spoke on serious subjects, but with a joke or two *in loco*, at the universities, at business gatherings, and at London dinners; I watched, lost in admiration, the inspired merriment of the Savages of Adelphi Terrace, and in my moments of leisure I observed, with a scientific eye, the gaieties of the London revues. As a result of which I say with conviction that, speaking by and large, the two communities are on the same level. A Harvard audience, as I have reason gratefully to acknowledge, is wonderful. But an Oxford audience is just as good. A gathering of businessmen in a textile town in the Midlands is just as heavy as a gathering of businessmen in Decatur, Indiana, but no heavier; and an audience of English schoolboys as at Rugby or at Clifton is capable of a wild and sustained merriment not to be outdone from Halifax to Los Angeles.

There is, however, one vital difference between American and English audiences which would be apt to discourage at the outset any American lecturer who might go to England. The English audiences, from the nature of the way in which they have been brought together, *expect more*. In England they still associate lectures with information. We don't. Our American lecture audiences are, in nine cases out of ten, organized by a woman's club of some kind and drawn not from the working class, but from—what shall we call it?— the class that doesn't have to work, or at any rate, not too hard. It is largely a social audience, well educated without being "highbrow," and tolerant and kindly to a degree. In fact, what the people mainly want is to see the lecturer. They have heard all about G. K. Chesterton and Hugh Walpole and John Drinkwater, and so when these gentlemen come to town the woman's club want to have a look at them, just as the English people, who are all crazy about animals, flock to the zoo to look at a new giraffe. They don't expect the giraffe to do anything in particular. They want to see it, that's all. So with the American woman's club audience. After they have seen Mr Chesterton they ask one another as they come out— just as an incidental matter—"Did you understand his lecture?" and the answer is, "I can't say that I did." But there is no malice about it. They can now go and say that they have *seen* Mr Chesterton; that's worth two dollars in itself. The nearest thing to this attitude of mind that I heard of in England was at the City Temple in London, where they have every week a huge gathering of about two thousand people, to listen to a (so-called) popular lecture. When I was there I was told that the person who had preceded me was Lord Haldane, who had lectured on Einstein's theory of relativity. I said to the chairman, "Surely this kind of audience couldn't understand a lecture like that!" He shook his head. "No," he said, *"they didn't understand it, but they all enjoyed it."*

I don't mean to imply by what I said above that American lecture audiences do not appreciate good things or that the English lecturers who come to this continent are all giraffes. On the contrary: when the audience finds that Chesterton and Walpole and Drinkwater, in addition to being *visible*, are also singularly interesting lecturers, they are all the better pleased. But this doesn't alter the fact that they have come primarily to *see the lecturer*.

Not so in England. Here a lecture (outside London) is organized on a much sterner footing. The people are there for information. The lecture is organized not by idle, amiable, charming women, but by a body called, with variations, the Philosophical Society. From experience I should define an English Philosophical Society as all the people in town who don't know anything about philosophy. The academic and university classes are never there. The audience is only of plainer folk. In the United States and Canada at any evening lecture a large sprinkling of the audience are in evening dress. At an English lecture (outside of London) none of them are; philosophy is not to be wooed in such a garb. Nor are there the same commodious premises, the same bright lights, and the same atmosphere of gaiety as at a society lecture in America. On the contrary, the setting is a gloomy one. In England, in winter, night begins at four in the afternoon. In the manufacturing towns of the Midlands and the north (which is where the philosophical societies flourish) there is always a drizzling rain and wet slop underfoot, a bedraggled poverty in the streets, and a dimness of lights that contrasts with the glare of light in an American town. There is no visible sign in the town that a lecture is to happen, no placards, no advertisements, nothing. The lecturer is conducted by a chairman through a side door in a dingy building (the Institute, established 1840), and then all of a sudden in a huge, dim hall—there sits the Philosophical Society. There are a thousand of them, but they sit as quiet as a prayer meeting. They are waiting to be fed—on information.

Now I don't mean to say that the Philosophical Society are not a good audience. In their own way they're all right. Once the Philosophical Society has decided that a lecture is humorous they do not stint their laughter. I have had many times the satisfaction of seeing a Philosophical Society swept away from its moorings and tossing in a sea of laughter, as generous and as whole-hearted as anything we ever see in America.

But they are not so willing to begin. With us

the chairman has only to say to the gaily dressed members of the Ladies' Fortnightly Club, "Well, ladies, I'm sure we are all looking forward very much to Mr Walpole's lecture," and at once there is a ripple of applause, and a responsive expression on a hundred charming faces.

Not so the Philosophical Society of the Midlands. The chairman rises. He doesn't call for silence. It is there, thick. "We have with us tonight," he says, "a man whose name is well known to the Philosophical Society" (*here he looks at his card*), "Mr Stephen Leacock." (*Complete silence.*) "He is a professor of political economy at—" Here he turns to me and says, "Which college did you say?" I answer quite audibly in the silence, "At McGill." "He is at McGill," says the chairman. (*More silence.*) "I don't suppose, however, ladies and gentlemen, that he's come here to talk about political economy." This is meant as a jest, but the audience takes it as a threat. "However, ladies and gentlemen, you haven't come here to listen to me" (*this evokes applause, the first of the evening*), "so without more ado" (*the man always has the impression that there's been a lot of "ado," but I never see any of it*) "I'll now introduce Mr Leacock." (*Complete silence.*)

Nothing of which means the least harm. It only implies that the Philosophical Society are true philosophers in accepting nothing unproved. They are like the man from Missouri. They want to be shown. And undoubtedly it takes a little time, therefore, to rouse them. I remember listening with great interest to Sir Michael Sadler, who is possessed of a very neat wit, introducing me at Leeds. He threw three jokes, one after the other, into the heart of a huge, silent audience without effect. He might as well have thrown soap bubbles. But the fourth joke broke fair and square like a bomb in the middle of the Philosophical Society and exploded them into convulsions. The process is very like what artillery men tell of "bracketing" the object fired at, and then landing fairly on it.

In what I have just written about audiences I have purposely been using the word English and not British, for it does not in the least apply to the Scotch. There is, for a humorous lecturer, no better audience in the world than a Scotch audience. The old standing joke about the Scotch sense of humour is mere nonsense. Yet one finds it everywhere.

"So you're going to try to take humour up to Scotland," the most eminent author in England said to me. "Well, the Lord help you. You'd better take an axe with you to open their skulls; there is no other way." How this legend started I don't know, but I think it is because the English are jealous of the Scotch. They got into the Union with them in 1707 and they can't get out. The Scotch don't want Home Rule, or Swa Raj, or Dominion status, or anything; they just want the English. When they want money they go to London and make it; if they want literary fame they sell their books to the English; and to prevent any kind of political trouble they take care to keep the Cabinet well filled with Scotchmen. The English for shame's sake can't get out of the Union, so they retaliate by saying that the Scotch have no sense of humour. But there's nothing in it. One has only to ask any of the theatrical people and they will tell you that the audiences in Glasgow and Edinburgh are the best in the British Isles—possess the best taste and the best ability to recognize what is really good.

The reason for this lies, I think, in the well-known fact that the Scotch are a truly educated people, not educated in the mere sense of having been made to go to school, but in the higher sense of having acquired an interest in books and a respect for learning. In England the higher classes alone possess this, the working class as a whole know nothing of it. But in Scotland the attitude is universal. And the more I reflect upon the subject, the more I believe that what counts most in the appreciation of humour is not nationality, but the degree of education enjoyed by the individual concerned. I do not think that there is any doubt that educated people possess a far wider range of humour than the uneducated class. Some people, of course, get overeducated and become hopelessly academic. The word "highbrow" has been invented exactly to fit the case. The sense of humour in the highbrow has become atrophied, or, to vary the metaphor, it is submerged or buried under the accumulated strata of his education, on the top soil of which flourishes a fine growth of conceit. But even in the highbrow the educated appreciation of humour is there—way down. Generally, if one attempts to amuse a highbrow he will resent it as if the process were beneath him; or perhaps the intellectual jealousy and touchiness with which he is always overcharged will lead him to retaliate with a pointless story from

Plato. But if the highbrow is right off his guard and has no jealousy in his mind, you may find him roaring with laughter and wiping his spectacles, with his sides shaking, and see him converted as by magic into the merry, clever little schoolboy that he was thirty years ago, before his education ossified him.

But with the illiterate and the rustic no such process is possible. His sense of humour may be there as a *sense*, but the mechanism for setting it in operation is limited and rudimentary. Only the broadest and most elementary forms of joke can reach him. The magnificent mechanism of the art of words is, quite literally, a sealed book to him. Here and there, indeed, a form of fun is found so elementary in its nature and yet so excellent in execution that it appeals to all alike, to the illiterate and to the highbrow, to the peasant and the professor. Such, for example, are the antics of Mr Charles Chaplin or the depiction of Mr Jiggs by the pencil of George McManus. But such cases are rare. As a rule the cheap fun that excites the rustic to laughter is execrable to the man of education.

In the light of what I have said before it follows that the individuals that are findable in every English or American audience are much the same. All those who lecture or act are well aware that there are certain types of people that are always to be seen somewhere in the hall. Some of these belong to the general class of discouraging people. They listen in stolid silence. No light of intelligence ever gleams on their faces; no response comes from their eyes.

I find, for example, that wherever I go there

is always seated in the audience, about three seats from the front, a silent man with a big motionless face like a melon. He is always there. I have seen that man in every city from Richmond, Indiana, to Bournemouth in Hampshire. He haunts me. I get to expect him. I feel like nodding to him from the platform. And I find that all other lecturers have the same experience. Wherever they go a man with the big face is always there. He never laughs; no matter if the people all round him are convulsed with laughter, he sits there like a rock—or, no, like a toad—immovable. What he thinks I don't know. Why he comes to lectures I cannot guess. Once, and once only, I spoke to him, or rather, he spoke to me. I was coming out from the lecture and found myself close to him in the corridor. It had been a rather gloomy evening; the audience had hardly laughed at all; and I know nothing sadder than a humorous lecture without laughter. The man with the big face, finding himself beside me, turned and said, "Some of them people weren't getting that tonight." His tone of sympathy seemed to imply that he had got it *all* himself; if so, he must have swallowed it whole without a sign. But I have since thought that this man with the big face may have his own internal form of appreciation. This much, however, I know: to look at him from the platform is fatal. One sustained look into his big, motionless face and the lecturer would be lost; inspiration would die upon one's lips—the basilisk isn't in it with him.

Personally, I no sooner see the man with the big face than instinctively I turn my eyes away. I look round the hall for another man that I know is always there, the opposite type, the little man with the spectacles. There he sits, good soul, about twelve rows back, his large spectacles beaming with appreciation and his quick face anticipating every point. I imagine him to be by trade a minor journalist or himself a writer of sorts, but with not enough of success to have spoiled him.

There are other people always there, too. There is the old lady who thinks the lecture improper; it doesn't matter how moral it is, she's out for impropriety and she can find it anywhere. Then there is another very terrible man against whom American lecturers in England should be warned—the man who is leaving on the 9 P.M. train. English railways running into suburbs and nearby towns have a schedule which is expressly arranged to have the principal train leave before the lecture ends. Hence the 9-P.M.-train man. He sits right near the front, and at ten minutes to nine he gathers up his hat, coat, and umbrella very deliberately, rises with great calm, and walks firmly away. His air is that of a man who has stood all that he can and can bear no more. Till one knows about this man, and the others who rise after him, it is very disconcerting; at first I thought I must have said something to reflect upon the royal family. But presently the lecturer gets to understand that it is only the nine o'clock train and that all the audience know about it. Then it's all right. It's just like the people rising and stretching themselves after the seventh innings in baseball.

In all that goes above I have been emphasizing the fact that the British and American sense of humour are essentially the same thing. But there are, of course, peculiar differences of form and peculiar preferences of material that often make them seem to diverge widely.

By this I mean that each community has, within limits, its own particular ways of being funny and its own particular conception of a joke. Thus, a Scotchman likes best a joke which he has all to himself or which he shares reluctantly with a few; the thing is too rich to distribute. The American loves particularly as his line of joke an anecdote with the point all concentrated at the end and exploding in a phrase. The Englishman loves best as his joke the narration of something that actually did happen and that depends, of course, for its point on reality.

There are plenty of minor differences, too, in point of mere form, and very naturally each community finds the particular form used by the others less pleasing than its own. In fact, for this very reason each people is apt to think its own humour the best.

Thus, on our side of the Atlantic, to cite our own faults first, we still cling to the supposed humour of bad spelling. We have, indeed, told ourselves a thousand times over that bad spelling is not funny, but is very tiresome. Yet it is no sooner laid aside and buried than it gets resurrected. I suppose the real reason is that it *is* funny, at least to our *eyes*. When Bill Nye spells wife with "yph" we can't help being amused. Now Bill Nye's bad spelling had absolutely no point to it except its oddity. At times it was extremely funny, but as a mode it led easily to widespread and pointless imitation. It was the kind of thing—like poetry—that anybody can do badly. It was most deservedly abandoned with execration. No American editor would print it today. But witness the new and excellent effect produced with bad spelling by Mr Ring W. Lardner. Here, however, the case is altered; it is not the *falseness* of Mr Lardner's spelling that is the amusing feature of it, but the *truth* of it. When he writes, *"dear friend, Al, I would of rote sooner,"* etc., he is truer to actual sound and intonation than the lexicon. The mode is excellent. But the imitations will soon debase it into such bad coin that it will fail to pass current. In England, however, the humour of bad spelling does not and has never, I believe, flourished. Bad spelling is only used in England as an attempt to reproduce phonetically a dialect; it is not intended that the spelling itself should be thought funny, but the dialect that it represents. But the effect, on the whole, is tiresome. A little dose of the humour of Lancashire or Somerset or Yorkshire pronunciation may be all right, but a whole page of it looks like the gibbering of chimpanzees set down on paper.

In America also we run perpetually to the (supposed) humour of slang, a form not used in England. If we were to analyse what we mean by slang I think it would be found to consist of the introduction of new metaphors or new forms of language of a metaphorical character, strained almost to the breaking point. Sometimes we do it with a single word. When some genius discovers that a "hat" is really only a "lid" placed on top of a human being, straightway the word "lid" goes rippling over the continent. Similarly a woman becomes a "skirt," and so on *ad infinitum*.

184

These words presently either disappear or else retain a permanent place, being slang no longer. No doubt half our words, if not all of them, were once slang. Even within our own memory we can see the whole process carried through; "cinch" once sounded funny; it is now standard American-English. But other slang is made up of descriptive phrases. At the best, these slang phrases are—at least we think they are—extremely funny. But they are funniest when newly coined, and it takes a master hand to coin them well. For a supreme example of wild vagaries of language used for humour, one might take O. Henry's "Gentle Grafter." But here the imitation is as easy as it is tiresome. The invention of pointless slang phrases without real suggestion or merit is one of our most familiar forms of factory-made humour. Now the English people are apt to turn away from the whole field of slang. In the first place it puzzles them—they don't know whether each particular word or phrase is a sort of idiom already known to Americans, or something (as with O. Henry) never said before and to be analysed for its own sake. The result is that with the English public the great mass of American slang writing (genius apart) doesn't go. I have even found English people of undoubted literary taste repelled from such a master as O. Henry (now read by millions in England) because at first sight they get the impression that it is "all American slang."

Another point in which American humour, or at least the form which it takes, differs notably from British, is in the matter of story telling. It was a great surprise to me the first time I went out to a dinner party in London to find that my host did not open the dinner by telling a funny story; that the guests did *not* then sit silent trying to "think of another"; that someone did not presently break silence by saying, "I heard a good one the other day"—and so forth. And I realized that in this respect English society is luckier than ours.

It is my candid opinion that no man ought to be allowed to tell a funny story or anecdote without a licence. We insist rightly enough that every taxi driver must have a licence, and the same principle should apply to anybody who proposes to act as a *raconteur*. Telling a story is a difficult thing—quite as difficult as driving a taxi. And the risks of failure and accident and the unfortunate consequences of such to the public, if not exactly identical, are, at any rate, analogous.

This is a point of view not generally appreciated. A man is apt to think that just because he has heard a good story he is able and entitled to repeat it. He might as well undertake to do a snake dance merely because he has seen Madame Pavlova do one. The point of a story is apt to lie in the telling, or at least to depend upon it in a high degree. Certain stories, it is true, depend so much on the final point, or "nub," as we Americans call it, that they are almost fool-proof. But even these can be made so prolix and tiresome, can be so messed up with irrelevant detail, that the general effect is utter weariness relieved by a kind of shock at the end. Let me illustrate what I mean by a story with a "nub" or point. I will take one of the best known, so as to make no claim for originality—for example, the famous anecdote of the man who wanted to be "put off at Buffalo." Here it is:

A man entered a sleeping-car and said to the porter, "At what time do we get to Buffalo?" The porter answered, "At half-past three in the morning, sir." "All right," the man said; "now I want to get off at Buffalo, and I want you to see that I get off. I sleep heavily and I'm hard to rouse. But you just make me wake up, don't mind what I say, don't pay attention if I kick about it, just *put me off*, do you see?" "All right, sir," said the porter. The man got into his berth and fell fast asleep. He never woke or moved till it was broad daylight and the train was a hundred miles beyond Buffalo. He called angrily to the porter, "See here, you, didn't I tell you to put me off at Buffalo?" The porter looked at him, aghast. "Well, I declare to goodness, boss!" he exclaimed; "if it wasn't you, who *was that man that I threw off this train at half-past three at Buffalo?*"

Now this story is as nearly fool-proof as can be. And yet it is amazing how badly it can be messed up by a person with a special gift for mangling a story. He does it something after this fashion:

"There was a fellow got on the train one night and he had a berth reserved for Buffalo; at least the way I heard it, it was Buffalo, though I guess, as a matter of fact, you might tell it on any other town just as well— or no, I guess he didn't have his berth reserved, he got on the train and asked the porter for a reservation for Buffalo—or, anyway, that part doesn't matter—say that he had a berth for Buffalo or any other place, and the porter came through and said, 'Do you want an early call?'—or no, he *went* to the porter—that was it—and said—"

But stop. The rest of the story becomes a mere painful waiting for the end.

Of course the higher type of funny story is the one that depends for its amusing quality not on the final point, or not solely on it, but on the wording and the narration all through. This is the way in which a story is told by a comedian or a person who is a *raconteur* in the real sense. When Sir Harry Lauder narrates an incident, the telling of it is funny from beginning to end. When some lesser person tries to repeat it afterwards, there is nothing left but the final point. The rest is weariness.

As a consequence most story-tellers are driven to telling stories that depend on the point or "nub" and not on the narration. The story-teller gathers these up till he is equipped with a sort of little repertory of fun by which he hopes to surround himself with social charm. In America especially (by which I mean here the United States and Canada, but not Mexico) we suffer from the story-telling habit. As far as I am able to judge, English society is not pervaded and damaged by the story-telling habit as much as is society in the United States and Canada. On our side of the Atlantic story-telling at dinners and on every other social occasion has become a curse. In every phase of social and intellectual life one is haunted by the funny anecdote. Anyone who has ever attended a Canadian or American banquet will recall the solemn way in which the chairman rises and says:

"Gentlemen, it is to me a very great pleasure and a very great honour to preside at this annual dinner. There was an old darky once—" and so forth. When he concludes he says, "I will now call upon the Reverend Dr Stooge, Head of the Provincial University, to propose the toast 'Our Dominion.'" Dr Stooge rises amid great applause and with great solemnity begins, "There were once two Irishmen—" and so on to the end. But in London, England, it is apparently not so. Not long ago I had the pleasure of meeting at dinner a member of the Government. I fully anticipated that as a member of the Government he would be expected to tell a funny story about an old darky, just as he would on our side of the water. In fact, I should have supposed that he could hardly get into the Government unless he did tell a funny story of some sort. But all through dinner the Cabinet Minister never said a word about either a Methodist minister, or a commercial traveller, or an old darky, or two Irishmen, or any of the stock characters of the American repertory. On another occasion I dined with a bishop of the Church. I expected that when the soup came he would say, "There was an old darky—" After which I should have had to listen with rapt attention, and, when he had finished, without any pause, rejoin, "There were a couple of Irishmen once—" and so on. But the bishop never said a word of the sort.

I can further, for the sake of my fellow-men in Canada and the United States who may think of going to England, vouchsafe the following facts: If you meet a director of the Bank of England, he does not say: "I am very glad to meet you. Sit down. There was a mule in Arkansas once," etc. How they do their banking without that mule I don't know. But they manage it. I can certify also that if you meet the proprietor of a great newspaper he will not begin by saying, "There was a Scotchman once." In fact, in England, you can mingle freely in general society without being called upon either to produce a funny story or to suffer from one.

I don't mean to deny that the American funny story, in capable hands, *is* amazingly funny and that it does brighten up human intercourse. But the real trouble lies, not in the fun of the story, but in the painful waiting for the point to come and in the strained and anxious silence that succeeds it. Each person around the dinner table is trying to "think of another." There is a dreadful pause. The hostess puts up a prayer that someone may "think of another." Then at last, to the relief of everybody, someone says: "I heard a story the other day —I don't know whether you've heard it—" And the grateful cries of "No! no! go ahead" show how great the tension has been.

Nine times out of ten the people have heard the story before; and ten times out of nine the teller damages it in the telling. But his hearers are grateful to him for having saved them from the appalling mantle of silence and introspection which had fallen upon the table. For the trouble is that when once two or three stories have been told it seems to be a point of honour not to subside into mere conversation. It seems rude, when a story-teller has at last reached the triumphant ending and climax of the mule from Arkansas, it seems impolite, to follow it up by saying, "I see that Germany refuses to pay the indemnity." It can't be done. Either the mule or the indemnity—you can't have both.

The English, I say, have not developed the American custom of the funny story as a form of social intercourse. But I do not mean to say that they are sinless in this respect. As I see it, they hand round in general conversation something nearly as bad in the form of what one may call the literal anecdote or personal experience. By this I refer to the habit of narrating some silly little event that has actually happened to them or in their sight, which they designate as "screamingly funny," and which was perhaps very funny when it happened but which is not the least funny in the telling. The American funny story is imaginary. It never happened. Somebody presumably once made it up. It is fiction. Thus there must once have been some great palpitating brain, some glowing imagination, which invented the story of the man who was put off at Buffalo. But the English "screamingly funny" story is not imaginary. It really did happen. It is an actual personal experience. In short, it is not fiction but history.

I think—if one may say it with all respect—that in English society girls and women are especially prone to narrate these personal experiences as contributions to general merriment rather than the men. The English girl has a sort of traditional idea of being amusing; the English man cares less about it. He prefers facts to fancy every time, and as a rule is free from that desire to pose as a humorist which haunts the American mind. So it comes about that most of the "screamingly funny" stories are told in English society by the women. Thus the counterpart of "put me off at Buffalo" done into English would be something like this: "We were *so* amused the other night in the sleeping-car going to Buffalo. There was the most amusing old Negro making the beds, a perfect scream, you know, and he kept *insisting* that if we wanted to get up at Buffalo we must all go to bed at nine o'clock. He positively wouldn't *let* us sit up—I mean to say it was killing the way he wanted to put us to bed. We all roared!"

Please note that *roar* at the end of the English personal anecdote. It is the sign that indicates that the story is over. When you are assured by the narrators that all the persons present "roared" or "simply roared," then you can be quite sure that the humorous incident is closed and that laughter is in place.

Now, as a matter of fact, the scene with the darky porter may have been, when it really happened, most amusing. But not a trace of it gets over in the story. There is nothing but the bare assertion that it was "screamingly funny" or "simply killing." But the English are such an honest people that when they say this sort of thing they believe one another and they laugh.

But, after all, why should people insist on telling funny stories at all? Why not be content to buy the works of some really first-class humorist and read them aloud in proper humility of mind without trying to emulate them? Either that or talk theology.

On my own side of the Atlantic I often marvel at our extraordinary tolerance and courtesy to one another in the matter of story-telling. I have never seen a bad story-teller thrown forcibly out of the room or even stopped and warned; we listen with the most wonderful patience to the worst of narration. The story is always without any interest except in the unknown *point* that will be brought in later. But this, until it does come, is no more interesting than tomorrow's breakfast. Yet for some reason or other we permit this story-telling habit to invade and damage our whole social life. The English always criticize this and I think they are absolutely right. To my mind in their social life they give the "funny story" its proper place and room and no more. That is to say—if ten people draw their chairs in to the dinner table and somebody really has just heard a story and wants to tell it, there is no reason against it. If he says, "Oh, by the way, I heard a good story today," it is just as if he said, "Oh, by the way, I heard a piece of news about John Smith." It is quite admissible as conversation. But he doesn't sit down to try to think, along with nine other rival thinkers, of all the stories that he had heard, and that makes all the difference.

The Scotch, by the way, resemble us in liking to tell and hear stories. But they have their own line. They like the stories to be grim, dealing in a jocose way with death and funerals. The story begins (will the reader kindly turn it into Scotch pronunciation for himself), "There was a Sandy MacDonald had died and the wife had the body all laid out for burial and dressed up very fine in his best suit," etc. Now for me that beginning is enough. To me that is not a story, but a tragedy. I am so sorry for Mrs MacDonald that I can't think of anything else. But I think the explanation is that the

Scotch are essentially such a devout people and live so closely within the shadow of death itself that they may without irreverence or pain jest where our lips would falter. Or else, perhaps they don't care a cuss whether Sandy MacDonald died or not. Take it either way.

But I am tired of talking of *our* faults. Let me turn to the more pleasing task of discussing those of the English. In the first place, and as a minor matter of form, I think that English humour suffers from the tolerance afforded to the pun. For some reason English people find puns funny. We don't. Here and there, no doubt, a pun may be made that for some exceptional reason becomes a matter of genuine wit. But the great mass of the English puns that disfigure the Press every week are mere pointless verbalisms that to the American mind cause nothing but weariness.

But even worse than the use of puns is the peculiar pedantry, not to say priggishness, that haunts the English expression of humour. To make a mistake in a Latin quotation or to stick on a wrong ending to a Latin word is not really an amusing thing. To an ancient Roman, perhaps, it might be. But then we are not ancient Romans; indeed, I imagine that if an ancient Roman could be resurrected, all the Latin that any of our classical scholars can command would be about equivalent to the French of a cockney waiter on a Channel steamer. Yet one finds even the immortal *Punch* citing recently as a very funny thing a newspaper misquotation of *"urbis et orbis"* instead of *"urbi et orbos,"* or the other way round. I forget which. Perhaps there was some further point in it that I didn't see, but, anyway, it wasn't funny. Neither is it funny if a person, instead of saying Archimedes, says Archimeeds; why shouldn't it have been Archimeeds? The English scale of values in these things is all wrong. Very few Englishmen can pronounce Chicago properly and they think nothing of that. But if a person mispronounces the name of a Greek village of what O. Henry called "The Year B.C." it is supposed to be excruciatingly funny.

I think in reality that this is only a part of the overdone scholarship that haunts so much of English writing—not the best of it, but a lot of it. It is too full of allusions and indirect references to all sorts of extraneous facts. The English writer finds it hard to say a plain thing in a plain way. He is too anxious to show in every sentence what a fine scholar he is. He carries in his mind an accumulated treasure of quotations, allusions, and scraps and tags of history, and into this, like Jack Horner, he must needs "stick in his thumb and pull out a plum." Instead of saying, "It is a fine morning," he prefers to write, "This is a day of which one might say with the melancholy Jacques, it is a fine morning."

Hence it is that many plain American readers find English humour "highbrow." Just as the English are apt to find our humour "slangy" and "cheap," so we find theirs academic and heavy. But the difference, after all, is of far less moment than might be supposed. It lies only on the surface. Fundamentally, as I said in starting, the humour of the two peoples is of the same kind and on an equal level.

There is one form of humour which the English have more or less to themselves, nor do I envy it to them. I mean the merriment that they appear able to draw out of the criminal courts. To me a criminal court is a place of horror, and a murder trial the last word in human tragedy. The English criminal courts I know only from the newspapers and ask no nearer acquaintance. But according to the newspapers the courts, especially when a murder case is on, are enlivened by flashes of judicial and legal humour that seem to meet with general approval. The current reports in the Press run like this:

"The prisoner, who is being tried on a charge of having burned his wife to death in a furnace, was placed in the dock and gave his name as Evans. 'Did he say Evans or Ovens?' asked Mr Justice Blank. The court broke into a roar, in which all joined but the prisoner. . . ." Or take this: "How many years did you say you served the last time?" asked the judge. "Three," said the prisoner. "Well, twice three is six," said the judge, laughing till his sides shook; "so I'll give you six years."

I don't say that those are literal examples of the humour of the criminal court. But they are close to it. For a judge to joke is as easy as it is for a schoolmaster to joke in his class. His unhappy audience has no choice but laughter. No doubt in point of intellect the English judges and the bar represent the most highly trained product of the British Empire. But when it comes to fun, they ought not to pit themselves against the unhappy prisoner. Why not take a man of their own size? For true amusement Mr Charles Chaplin or Mr Leslie Henson could give them sixty in a hundred. I even think I could myself.

One final judgement, however, might with due caution be hazarded. I do not think that, on the whole, the English are quite as fond of humour as we are. I mean they are not so willing to welcome at all times the humorous point of view as we are in America. The English are a serious people, with many serious things to think of—football, horse racing, dogs, fish, and many other concerns that demand much national thought: they have so many national preoccupations of this kind that they have less need for jokes than we have. They have higher things to talk about, whereas on our side of the water, except when the World's Series is being played, we have few, if any, truly national topics.

And yet I know that many people in England would exactly reverse this last judgement and say that the Americans are a desperately serious people. That in a sense is true. Any American who takes up with an idea such as New Thought, Psychoanalysis or Eating Sawdust, or any "uplift" of any kind becomes desperately lopsided in his seriousness, and as a very large number of us cultivate New Thought, or practise breathing exercises, or eat sawdust, no doubt the English visitors think us a desperate lot.

Anyway, it's an ill business to criticize another people's shortcomings. What I said at the start was that the British are just as humorous as are the Americans, or the Canadians, or any of us across the Atlantic, and for greater certainty I repeat it at the end.

THE AUTHOR

Stephen Leacock was born in 1869 at Swanmore in Hampshire, England. In 1876 the family emigrated to Canada and settled on a farm near Lake Simcoe. Educated at Upper Canada College and the University of Toronto, Stephen Leacock taught first at his own old school of Upper Canada and later at McGill University in Montreal, where he rose to be head of the department of economics and political science. His first writings dealt with economics and Canadian history, but gradually as his true genius emerged he grew further and further away from the field and was attracted into his natural element of pure fun. Now he is remembered mainly as a humorist and the author of close to forty books of nonsense, including *Literary Lapses, Nonsense Novels, Sunshine Sketches of a Little Town, Behind the Beyond, Moonbeams from the Larger Lunacy, Frenzied Fiction, Short Circuits, Helements of Hickonomics, Our British Empire, Over the Footlights,* and *Arcadian Adventures with the Idle Rich*. At the time of his death in 1944, Leacock left four completed chapters of what was to have been his autobiography. These were published posthumously under the title *The Boy I Left Behind Me*. In 1946 it was decided by the Leacock Society to present a silver medal annually to the best book of humour published in Canada during the year. The Leacock Medal has become one of the outstanding awards in the literary world.

THE NEW CANADIAN LIBRARY